LOST AND THEN FOUND

LOST AND THEN FOUND

Turning Life's Disappointments Into Hidden Treasures

Dr Trevor Griffiths

paternoster
press

Copyright © 1999

First published in 1999 by Paternoster Press

05 04 03 02 01 00 99   7 6 5 5 4 3 2 1

Paternoster Press is an imprint of Paternoster Publishing,
PO Box 300, Carlisle, Cumbria, CA3 0QS, UK
http://www.paternoster-publishing.com

The right of Trevor Griffiths to be identified as the Author of
this Work has been asserted by him in accordance with
Copyright, Designs and Patents Act 1988.

British Library Cataloguing in Publication Data

A catalogue record for this book is available from the
British Library

ISBN 0-85364-966-9

Cover Design by Mainstream, Lancaster
Typeset by WestKey Ltd, Falmouth, Cornwall
Printed in Great Britain by
Caledonian International Book Manufacturing Ltd, Glasgow

Contents

This book is dedicated to my wife Marian and
to my daughters Abigail and Tamsin,
who have all made their loss reactions known
in so many different ways
whenever I switched on the word processor.

Acknowledgements

I am indebted to the research of Elisabeth Kübler-Ross on bereavement which resulted in the framework which is applied in a more general way in this book. Her approach is outlined in her books, *On Death and Dying* (1969) and, *Death – The Final Stage of Growth* (1975). My gratitude also goes out to numerous colleagues in medicine and clinical psychology who have offered comments while the method was being developed. In particular I would like to mention Dr Tony Carr of the Department of Psychology at the University of Plymouth whose specialist work on bereavement has contributed much clarity to some difficult areas. The readability and text flow of this book has been greatly helped by the reflective comments of James Rye. My particular thanks go to David Ames of 'Mission to Marriage' whose support and encouragement towards publication has enabled this book to be completed.

Introduction

This book is intended for those who know something is going wrong in their life or relationships, but who doubt that counselling is the right approach for them, or who cannot get the time to see a counsellor. It can also be used by counsellors and doctors to help their clients and patients through life events. The method has been used in my General Practice surgery for many years, and I have found it to be particularly acceptable to men, who often find it more difficult to talk about personal matters than women.

Parts of it are intended to be used as a workbook. One quick skim through it in an evening will introduce you to the key framework. This explains how some of our more unpleasant emotions fit into a process that leads through to a creative solution. The process takes time, but if we know where it is going the journey becomes a little easier.

You will gain a deeper understanding of the causes of your own loss of well-being and a greater insight into many relationship difficulties if you give the book a more thorough reading. The framework has proved to be powerful to unlock some difficult problems, so avoiding the need to see a counsellor while giving a way to prevent the same difficulties arising again in the future.

However, I need to give a word of warning. This book is not a magic wand but a work manual. Some couples have worked for over a year with this framework to understand the complexity of their relationship. The framework needs re-visiting again and again as each new situation needs to be re-interpreted in its terms. The book's method is to show how one emotion can evolve creatively into another, and how to use the framework to get talking about what is going on behind the emotions to help this process along. As we choose to use the type of language provided by this book, we can use it to calm a turbulent sea of emotions into a turning tide of relationships.

After a while, when the ideas and language have been worked into our general approach to life, this book can become like an item in a tool box or a kitchen drawer – something that can be taken out to be used whenever necessary to make life a little easier.

PART 1
RECOGNIZING LOSS

CHAPTER 1

Life Cycle

This book is about a common human experience. We all experience loss in various forms and at various times. These experiences of loss and the ways in which we respond to them are far more important than we may realize. I have two main aims in writing. First, I want to help readers spot the in-built reactions that we all have to the loss of anyone or anything, or to any hope or idea that is valuable to us. Secondly, I want the book to enable readers to gain insight into what happens when we try to ignore loss reactions and 'carry on regardless'. For these loss reactions, if they are ignored and hidden, usually add something harmful to our own behaviour, relationships and health; and possibly also to those of other people. They bring an additional element, and one which is uncomfortable, to the unpredictability of our shared human life.

The first two parts of the book lay out a framework for understanding these loss reactions and for understanding some of the various ways they can emerge from our hidden depths onto the surface of life. We can all see them if we choose to look. The third part of the book empowers the readers to use this framework to improve the range of choices they have to change their life circumstances for the benefit of all concerned.

Gathering and loss

In daily life, as autumn and winter follow spring and sum-
mer, so we respond to the changing seasons by giving up
our 'warm weather' ways of doing things and adopting
'cold weather' ways. As the song says, 'To everything –
turn, turn – there is a season.' Human life, whatever area
you choose to look at, is a continuous process of change
which may be thought of as involving 'gathering' and
'loss'.

In all this change we usually think our security lies in our
ability to 'gather' effectively. For example, as a father I feel
inordinately pleased that my work enables me to provide
money to buy the children's trainers. I gain satisfaction and
a sense of well-being from this experience of gathering,
and recognize in others the hidden loss when someone has
insufficient money to buy something they would like to
give. Likewise, organizing an outing for the family is a sort
of 'gathering' of resources, as is finding the tools and
equipment to replace a loose slate on the roof of my house.

But there are also experiences of 'loss'. One of the
secrets of well-being this book aims to open up is that I
need also to learn how to let go and effectively 'lose'. If
I cannot afford to go to Centre Parks for a holiday, am I
going to let the resentment spoil my day trips to the sea, or
instead make the most of our time together and prevent the
disappointment spreading to my children? If I cannot have
children, and medical treatment to conceive has failed, am
I going to ruin my marriage as well by self-criticism, or
apply to adopt instead and give what I can, recognizing
that adopted children will want to know, sooner or later,
who are their natural parents? How do we learn to handle
the feelings that come with these sorts of adjustments?
Although our initial reaction to the idea may be negative,
there is no shame in the wholeness of a life that has

inevitably included both gathering and losing. Indeed, accepting this truth and living by it can actually make us happier.

Have you ever had a feeling of need but also feel frustrated because you do not know what could meet that need? In that situation we may try various ways to substitute 'gain' for that sense of need, and attempt to gather all sorts of stimuli to help, but nothing seems to do the trick? That feeling of need may well be the result of our having 'lost' something without recognising it as a loss. What we need to gain in this situation is more insight into our loss reactions, so that we can finish grieving properly for whatever it is that we have lost.

Two halves make the whole truth

In order to understand this book it is important to take account of the kind of society for which it has been written.

Over the last two hundred years particularly, western culture has encouraged people to believe that it is our power to reason which can save us from this eternal cycle of life's gathering and loss. This is partly true. But it is only half true. We can indeed reason how to control the gathering half of the cycle of life, and we can even reason our way into preventing some loss, for a while. But to go through life believing that reason has the power to control all of our life is just about as dangerous as walking onto an overhanging cliff-top with a deep fall below.

As I write this, I recall the experience of some good friends of ours, a married couple, both of them doctors like my wife and me. I can remember their happiness when the wife became pregnant. But I also remember seeing her a few weeks after the birth. She was cuddling her crying baby. Yet she too was distraught, with tears streaming down her face.

As she cried she told us how she knew she was in a post-natal depression, how she knew all about post-natal depressions, how she had helped many of her patients through their post-natal depressions – but now she was utterly unable to stop herself feeling out of control and useless.

So what is the other half of truth, which our western culture often forgets and which mingles with the half truth that reason can save us? It is simply this: *love can save us*. Our modern western culture needs to re-learn that while reason is important in controlling 'gathering' particularly, love is important in limiting the harm of 'losing'. But loving by itself is not adequate. Showing love to me while I am grieving is important, but love itself may not enable me to pass through the grief in a helpful way. Certainly to know neighbourly or friendly love is a 'gain'; but only if this love can be a means of helping me to achieve acceptance of the loss will I eventually be able to move forward in a positive way.

The cultural taboo against talking about loss

Western culture tends to believe that our ability to reason through problems enlightens us – and that those who cannot reason are unenlightened. In the main people respect 'reasonable' self-control. Because reasoning is most powerful when it comes to 'gathering', this one-sided view of enlightenment has created its opposite, a new great taboo subject in western society. Sex was the great taboo subject; but with the development of birth control we now expect people to control and express their sexual instincts with reasonable skill. In its place the great unspoken taboo subjects, that are out of our reasoned control, have become death and loss.

Western culture feeds on immediate hope and cannot bear to anticipate loss other than to insure against it. I know an insurance agent well who is convinced that most people to whom he sells life policies believe they are not really going to die. Every day advertisers and script writers offer us so much to desire – from instant wealth to eternal youth – that it becomes more and more difficult to take our eyes off the 'gains' that we long for and face directly up to the ongoing 'losses' in our life.

Because so much entertainment is always available to distract us from the hurt within, it is easier now to hide from our own emotions than at any other time in the history of the world. Science has given us the hope of control, and fictional entertainment gives us the hope of fulfilment. Have you noticed that death and loss are the realities about which both science and entertainment have little positive to say?

Death and loss are taboo because we culturally have lost the skills needed to handle the instinctual reactions to loss that arise outside our control, and to turn them into something that creatively allows new life to flourish for ourselves and also for others. For example, I see it happen time and again that my grieving patients feel ostracized by their friends and neighbours. I have to explain that this is because these previously friendly people cannot face up to their own inadequacy, and fear that not you but they themselves will lose their emotional self-control which our culture respects. No amount of reasoning can help us through this dilemma; only neighbourly love.

The inability to think clearly about loss may itself be crippling western culture. Our failure here is bringing a sort of blindness into some of our relationships that we are unable to perceive even though we may be seeing some of the consequences as we watch the divorce statistics climb. One of the effects of unrecognized and unresolved loss reactions can be a numbing of sensitivity and a paralysis of responsiveness that makes us feel crippled inside. Reading and working through this book will help you to re-gain what you have lost in these areas of your life, without losing your reason also.

A question of attitude

For as long as we see life as a struggle between winning and losing, to lose will seem a failure and a threat to our survival. But losing a struggle is different to loss in the life cycle. The life cycle has a way of turning loss into something ultimately creative. Loss and choosing to give away are ultimately two sides of the same coin. The difference is in our attitude.

When all is said and done, adjusting to loss is basically the same as changing our attitude from one of the failure of losing into one of the creativity of making a mature positive choice to give, in the hope that it will ultimately bring life to others. An easy example would be my attitude as I watch my daughter mature into a young woman, whom I know will one day leave home. I can regard this as a crippling loss and berate her for the pain that her leaving will cause. Alternatively I can respect her independence, give her the freedom she will long for, be grateful for all she has given, and look forward to finding new ways of relating to her as my adult daughter, no longer as my child. More difficult to live with is my attitude when I suffer loss as a result of injustice or unrighteousness. For example, those who experience torture at the hands of a repressive political system must adjust to their powerlessness in the hope either, as bitterness, that one day there will be a balancing of the books or, better, that what endures of me, my relatedness despite loss, will enable the repressors eventually to find a new set of values to live by. We shall look more closely in Part 3 at the role of hope and relatedness in our living creatively with true acceptance of loss.

To live in the hope that our loss can ultimately bring life to others is simply said, but for most of us that is so fraught with risk that to hold onto hope, or to believe that hope can be re-born beyond our previous hopes, may be enormously difficult to achieve. Along the way we may feel instead like giving up, or like unloading our bad feelings onto other people, quite literally 'giving them grief'. But why does it happen?

A train of emotional reactions described below follows quite automatically whenever we experience loss or, as is often forgotten, encounter the risk of loss. These gut level reactions are part of our genetic survival mechanism. They are built into our inheritance. Automatic emotional responses, although unpleasant, are the very means by which we learn to adapt to the variety of circumstances we face, as we constantly re-make a zone in which our values survive and have a hope of a future. Because the choices we make follow *in the wake of* these very powerful instinctual reactions, making a positive response that respects others as much as ourselves is often difficult. When life gets tough and stressed, no matter how much we may wish to thrive with others in the security and pleasure of life's shared features, our automatic individualistic survival reactions will also be activated. For all sorts of very good reasons we may choose to try and ignore these innate survival loss reactions so as not to act them out. But we do so at our peril.

The framework presented in this book may help the reader to spot how you or others you relate to may be ignoring loss reactions, and how these hidden reactions might be harming behaviour, relationships and health. Then the key to healing change lies in recognizing these automatic loss reactions as they crop up, and rejecting the negative choices of ignoring them or destructively acting them out. The better way is the positive one of choosing to honestly talk them through.

The scope of loss reactions

Loss reactions are most profound and intense when somebody we love, dies. But we experience them in a variety of other contexts. It is important to see that even the risk of losing anything or anybody that we value will bring in its wake a loss reaction. It may be loss of our home, loss of our environment or community by moving away, loss of our job, status or income, loss of friends, loss of trust, loss of hope, loss of our car, loss of our favourite television programme, loss of a pet, loss of perfection, loss of a part of our body through injury of operation, even loss of our expectations that leads to disappointment. When we lose anything or any relationship that we value (or which values us) there is injury to our sense of identity.

This injury to our personal identity needs to heal just as much as an injury to our body needs to heal. If, for instance, you were injured in an accident and lost a leg, then the wound itself would go through various stages of healing, although complications may arise along the way to delay that. The emotional stages of a loss reaction are similar, in that complications can also arise to delay personal growth and healing. Personal losses may also very rapidly pile one on another. For example, there are more losses to recover from following such an accident than simply the leg itself. You would also discover how difficult it is to relearn how to balance and walk, and more than that you would have to relearn how to socialize confidently with people who will immediately identify that there is something odd about you.

When it is a physical loss it is relatively easy to identify the natural and automatic stages of healing from loss and the re-making of one's sense of identity. It is less easy to recognize the natural sequence of healing from injury to those intangible features of life, our patterns of relatedness which actually are our identity as a whole person. These features are just as real as a leg, only less visible. Like the wind, which we cannot see even though it can cause real damage, our relationships are real and their loss is real loss. If you talk to somebody who has lost a lifetime partner, they feel as if something has been torn away from every single cell of his or her body. Do not doubt that in true marriage two individuals become one in body as well as spirit, or you will be shocked at the depth of loss when one goes.

The loss of our relationship with something or somebody who is part of our identity leaves something like a raw surface to our soul. This wound will heal by a natural sequence of stages which we are aware of emotionally, much as the leg wound heals through a natural sequence of stages of which we are aware physically. Emotions partly are, after all, our internal chemistry of relationships at work, readjusting. It is not possible to skip any of these stages, though some may be processed quickly, and nothing can make loss a pleasant process to go through. Understanding the process does not make it any easier, but it can help to stop us getting stuck in any one stage and prolonging the hurt. And it can help us to realize how being stuck is affecting the way we get on with others while we are going through it, or why somebody else is being so difficult when they are going through it.

This book may show you a way to restore your skills to identify when loss is affecting relationships and your well-being. It is reasonable to hope that in so doing we may all become more neighbourly givers of life.

CHAPTER 2

Loss Reactions

Learning the loss reaction sequence by heart

We are all individuals. Just as people have different faces and differ in the ways they cope with growing up through the teenage years, so people also vary enormously in how swiftly or thoroughly they work through losses. There is no 'correct' way of experiencing loss. However, from the various ways of describing loss reactions I have selected the one presented here simply because I have always found it helpful. In using this model or pattern of experiencing loss I'm not trying to present a path that everyone should follow. You may think of it as being like a magnifying glass, or a camera or even a scanner. It can help give insight into what is going on in us at any particular time.

This helpful pattern sees people as adjusting to loss in seven stages: shock, denial, anger, guilt, bargaining, depression, and acceptance. It is worth trying to learn that sequence off by heart, and this is easier if you think of them as three pairs:

- shock and denial;
- anger and guilt;
- bargaining and depression . . . leading through to . . . *acceptance*.

If we can recall these stages, then when in some quiet moment we are reflecting on how we are feeling about any particular loss, we will be able to consider why we are stuck in one, or cannot face the next, or are going round a couple of them in a whirlpool of emotion. The real value of learning them as a sequence is that, having named the feeling, we see the creative direction to evolve is down the list, not back up it.

The seven stages of loss reactions

1. Shock

I remember visiting a patient a few moments after her brother had died and noticing the way she looked through me and seemed confused. It seemed strange at first that she wasn't weeping; but when suddenly something occurs completely out of context, our feelings may be numbed. We no longer know what to expect. We may get disorientated. This is the condition that underlies *shock*.

This kind of disorientation is quite common in normal life, but it is usually only a brief experience, after which – in normal life – a regular train of events generally follows the unexpected. We may be temporarily puzzled by a roar behind us, but this confusion disappears when we realize that the roar has been caused by a low flying aeroplane. But if no such understandable sequence follows the unusual event, our disorientation may last longer. The roar may remain unexplained and then becomes both puzzling and frightening. After we have experienced a severe loss, the only continuity between 'before' and 'after' may be the face which announced the bad news and which remains looking at us. This immovable face gradually pulls us reluctantly into a new reality that is not going to go away.

As we experience shock we may very likely also feel afraid. Fear often paralyses us – sometimes quite literally. In our minds we retreat, as we shrink from coping with the great unknown that has suddenly loomed before us. If we get stuck in this fear, it may convert into a free-floating sort of anxiety that colours our whole experience of life, turning every aspect sour. What were once routine tasks suddenly become very difficult because we are anxious about newness and failure. Meeting people too can become unexpectedly demanding because they also seem to bring the unexpected.

To be in shock is to be oppressed by doubt. We doubt that we have the resources to cope with change, which brings a fear of being overwhelmed. The doubt may recur every time something particularly distressing is recalled. Sometimes such a recall may be so brief that we are scarcely conscious of the memory. We know that suddenly we are feeling odd and 'out of it' – without knowing why.

2. *Denial*

Denial of loss is the hope that if we ignore it, it will just go away or sort itself out on its own.

Denial can be a reasonable and useful coping mechanism when life is full of responsibilities, so that considering the loss must be deferred until there is time to feel it. But denial can only ever be a temporary state of affairs; sooner or later the memory will return.

In many losses this may be a very brief stage. When we deny loss, the news of loss still comes towards us, but we somehow struggle to shield ourselves from it, not letting it really reach us and affect us. Husbands or wives who find that their partner has been involved in adultery go through a stage of not accepting that it has happened. It 'couldn't happen to them'. The loss of the faithfulness from their marriage is too challenging to accept easily.

As the *memory* of the loss returns, so do the *emotions* associated with it. The curious feature of denial is that the emotions of loss do not go away with time but sit there as if deep-frozen, awaiting the thaw. Years after denied losses these emotions can re-activate, and in such a case we may finally face up to the reality of the loss at a time when we have the energy and trust to integrate that loss into our experience without it destroying our identity.

3. *Anger*

When we truly realize that we are actually experiencing loss the first reaction is an automatic outburst of anger. We want to go out and prevent the loss. Anger is the drive to be assertive or constructively aggressive as we seek to influence the world out there and stop the loss from happening.

Seen in this light, anger is in fact a very creative emotion. We all need a bit of anger to hold our lives and the safety of our loved ones together in some sort of order. At first the anger may be nothing more than a shout. But as we re-live the memory and perhaps quickly plan our response, the anger phase in the face of risk of loss becomes an assertive and creative drive. The problems come when loss has actually occurred and cannot be prevented or restored, or when we have never learned how to express our anger in creative activity. If we fail to express it so, the drive will still remain – but what do we do with it then?

The anger tends to be directed, and may become vengeful, though often this amounts to no more than an outburst. It may be directed at somebody at the scene of an accident whom we may want to blame, but who was not the cause. More likely it will be directed towards the person we most love or trust, who may find our attitude extremely difficult to understand or cope with. The loved person may complicate the whole issue further by (understandably) responding in a self-justifying manner: 'Who does [s]he think [s]he is in talking to me like that? I was the one who was there to pick up the pieces when it first happened!' But in fact the person who is experiencing loss simply wants the loved one to hear the hurt, and is hoping that the loved one will still be around to help when the unpleasantness of the anger has gone.

The relatives of victims of rape or assault often convert their anger into fitting locks to all the doors of the house. They may also channel it into other overbearingly protective behaviour which is well organized, but also inappropriate, especially if it continues long after the event. But what else could they do with their anger? Sometimes, after particularly distressing accidents, some people will direct their anger into campaigning and organising in order to prevent a similar loss from afflicting anyone else.

From their childhood, some people have learned to conceal their anger because expressing it brought even worse trouble on them. To show strong emotion was unacceptable. For such people loss reactions may be extremely threatening because of this anger phase. They may repress their anger, pushing it down and directing it into the depths of their soul where they hope it can do no harm. Unfortunately the anger does not go away but becomes destructive, producing a poor sense of personal value and emerging eventually as a clinical depression.

Repressed anger is only one of several ways in which depressions arise. When this type of depression is treated, as the person emerges from it the anger then finds expression as part of the recovery phase. In fact it is simply loss reaction emotions thawing out after a period of denial. If the person facing loss and those around them have not been warned of this, it can be quite distressing and can be misinterpreted.

4. Guilt

Guilt is part of the price we pay for loving. One of the greatest tragedies I see in the surgery is when someone who has cared for an elderly relative for years, who has done everything to help them, then becomes guilt ridden after they have died. This can be a very difficult stage to work through, and we shall look at it further in later chapters.

When we lose someone we have emotionally bonded with, or if we lose something that we feel is part of our identity (such as a limb, or a job, or a marriage), we are likely to ask ourselves uncomfortable questions: 'What did I do to cause that loss?' or 'What could I have done to prevent that loss?' The drive so to question and criticize seems completely irrational, but it arouses strong emotions. Asking the two questions forms part of our drive to understand and to survive. The questioning is the way we learn: 'I may have lost that one, but I certainly am not going to lose the next one.' If we do not question, then we simply will not develop as people.

The problem with the guilt stage of loss is that the questions come with a horrible sense of wrongdoing. This *feeling* needs to be distinguished from the *questions* associated with it, because it is the questioning which is the real substance of the guilt stage. Most often the answers to both questions are simply, 'Nothing'. We need to understand that such questioning is legitimate, and that it is equally legitimate to answer, 'I did nothing wrong, but still I lost.' The feeling of wrongdoing, however, can drive people off on 'guilt trips' that harm them and also those close to them.

5. Bargaining

Bargaining can be a very tricky stage. It is basically a phase in which each and every possibility for restoring the loss is explored. We feel we must maintain the status quo and are determined to leave no stone unturned as we search for some deal to secure this end. The emotion which drives us to 'bargain' for the return of a loss is our yearning or longing to fill the emptiness the loss has caused. Yearning may be prolonged when someone has died but the options for bargaining are limited. Some people try to contact the dead as part of this phase, and many ask God to take them as well. If the loss is one where there is some real possibility of restoration this stage can indeed be very prolonged and troublesome. This may happen in a marital separation: one partner may make all sorts of promises to bring the other back, tying up their own life in impossible conditions which, even if the partner does return, are unsustainable. Thus the loss eventually recurs.

One reason why bargaining may become so complicated is that every time a possibility for restoring the loss is explored and fails, we realize once more that we are powerless to restore it. Consequently we experience another mini-loss reaction, with its accompanying feelings of fear, doubt, anger, guilt and yearning. This means that when bargaining is in progress, at any one time the emotions of loss become jumbled as they rage back and forth and pile one on another. This is particularly noticeable when people are diagnosed with life-threatening disease such as AIDS or cancer. They are literally bargaining for their lives. No clear sequence of loss reaction emotions can be identified because the emotions are all there together in a horrible mess. Some people eventually manage to assert their own wills and achieve authority over the mess; others succumb to it.

The bargaining phase slowly declines as the options to restore the loss fail one by one and we progressively realize the awful truth that we have no power over our loss. It is this sense of growing powerlessness that leads into the next phase.

6. *Depression*

The depression of loss is very different to the depression of repressed anger, and sometimes a doctor is needed to diagnose which one is having its effect because the approach to treatment may be different in the two cases. The depressive phase of loss may need no treatment other than reassurance that it is normal and not going to last forever nor drive the sufferer mad.

Depression of loss is the overbearing realization that the lost person or thing has gone forever and can never be retrieved. We are powerless and useless in the face of what has happened. Life has become valueless, meaningless, black, unsupportive, hopeless. There may be despair, a sense of alienation, or perhaps hostility if some anger remains. Nothing seems worthwhile. No sense of motivation moves us other than the needs of the day, and sometimes not even those. Any identity which we gained from association with the person or thing that has gone, is lost or crushed.

7. *Acceptance*

True acceptance arises gradually out of depression. Acceptance means realizing that even though the loss is permanent, and even though I have found a limit to my ability to control the world I am nevertheless still a creative person. Others do value me, even if only in certain ways (perhaps for my company, rather than my intellect). I realize that I can still have a creative effect when I express myself and seek change.

True acceptance is a very rich and mature state; although the memory of the loss may be with a person every day, they are still able to make new relationships and achieve a good life. Human beings are able to integrate joy and laughter with the sadness of loss without any inconsistency. We may indeed experience a sense of growing up in this maturity. As the adjustment to loss comes to completion, we increase in self-respect through accepting our limitations. In fact we re-structure our identity in this way. We begin to see ourselves as more all-rounded people. We mature, not through growing older, but as we learn to let go; as we learn to adopt a different perspective. Because our limitations are changing throughout our lives, and as we are always exploring our limitations, this acceptance of loss is an ongoing process which is at the very root of maturation throughout life.

There is a problem about 'acceptance'. Sometimes people think they have accepted losses, when in fact they are still denying them. A gentle rekindling of trust may be needed before people are willing to openly confront the denial mechanisms and underlying emotions that remain from the past. There is one way to tell the difference between true acceptance and denial. When the loss is remembered, in true acceptance there will be a genuine sense of sadness accompanying it. If the loss has been denied, however, then the memory of it will return with some of the harder emotions – shock, fear, doubt, anxiety, anger, guilt, yearning, despair, and so on.

Time to heal

The pattern of stages described above (I sometimes call them 'stepping stones' so we know where we are with them) appears time and again in subtly different guises depending on the nature of the loss:

- Doubting our resources to cope –
- Hoping it will go away –
- Striving to prevent loss, regardless –
- Questioning why I could not prevent it –
- Trying to restore it –

- Realizing I am powerless to do so – and –
- Relearning how to live, accepting my limits.

Movement forward does not happen by simply progressively working through the seven stages of shock and denial, anger and guilt, bargaining and depression to acceptance. What tends to happen is that whenever the loss is remembered people start right back at the beginning again. They rapidly move through from shock to however far they feel they have the emotional resources on that occasion. As time passes the 'stepping stones' become clearer and they tend to move on average through to, for example, guilty questioning rather than just anger. Later they may move rapidly through to depressive feelings, and so on, as the resources to cope with the earlier stages are more clearly known. But if new aspects of the loss are considered (perhaps something sparks a new, painful memory), the reaction may stop on an earlier stepping stone again. The person may appear to be getting worse, rather than better as they struggle to re-muster their resources for this new adjustment.

Major grief, such as for the death of a spouse or a child, may need even two years for the adjustments to work through. Recovery from major grief is usually not a process where the emotions get steadily less intense. Instead, over many months the intervals between the occasions on which the loss is remembered tend to get longer. But on those occasions the emotions can return with as much force as they ever had. Thus, even eighteen months after the loss, someone who has started to build new relationships and is able to laugh with others may hear a piece of music or see a familiar object and be suddenly reminded of the loss. Once more, tears will well up quickly and the old hurt return, but significantly, for a shorter time.

But what about all the minor losses of life which we try to push out of our minds? And what about all those losses which were significant for us but which mean nothing to other people who know us? How long does it take for these to work through to the extent that we can accept the limitations imposed by the loss while still being aware that we are valuable just as we are, and creative in all sorts of little ways? Perhaps it is all these unrecognized losses that reduce us to tears on those occasions when we do not know why, or that make us irritable with colleagues at work out of proportion to the objective situation – or them with us . . . And as all the small disappointments accumulate in the early stages of marriage, as we get to know more about each other, is separation and divorce really the only way of making the extent of our feelings of loss known before we have discovered how we really can be creative in each other's lives?

If we wish to move into a new territory we need to learn a new language. This loss reaction analysis is a language of emotion which can give us the resources we need to stop doubting ourselves and each other.

PART 2
REACTIONS TO LOSS

CHAPTER 3

Complicated Reactions when Several Losses come Close Together

Taking a risk to talk about past losses

For some strange reason the emotions of loss hibernate. They curl up and cool down and wait until the conditions are right before they come out. They will remain dormant until we allow ourselves time to reflect on our loss and adjustment.

When the emotions of loss hibernate, they are not non-existent. When we discover a hibernating hedgehog, we tend to feel surprise or shock and then re-cover it with leaves. We do the same with denied loss emotions. We actively avoid them, and respond in our unique manner as we re-cover that tender area of our soul. These unique denial mannerisms affect our behaviour in ways that others may see more clearly than we can. Perhaps it is the frantic activity, or the tightly pursed lips that give us away. These mannerisms can cause all sorts of problems in our relationships, until the time feels right to switch off denial and re-awaken to the harsh light of a new day.

When we do allow time for the hibernating emotions to re-surface, which may happen when we are alone or with somebody else, we face a risk. We may be swamped for a while by the powerful feelings. To express our feelings and thoughts about our loss may need a daring effort of will, and we risk losing the respect of others. Consequently, if somebody who is listening shows that he or she is embarrassed by, or cannot cope with the expression of our true feelings, we may not take the risk of expressing them again for a long time. We shun the awkwardness. We dared to bargain – 'I'll express true feelings if you listen and agree not to be shocked' – and lost.

This book has three main messages. The first of them is:

To help somebody else through their grief you do not need to say anything . . . Sometimes choose only to stick around and be a listening presence. That is showing true mercy.

Multiple losses are each worked through at a different speed

A friend of mine recently experienced five losses in rapid succession. He had to move to another part of the country, to a smaller house, because he had lost his job. His father died soon after the move. His daughter also left home to go to university. If several losses occur within a fairly short period of time like this then the situation can become very confused. The reason for this, is that we have to work separately through each loss until we reach acceptance. Each working through will have its own path, and own time scale. The processing of one loss may be interrupted by another. At any one time a person can be feeling angry about that loss, guilty about another, depressed about a third, denying yet another, and so on. In addition, each loss can involve a complex bargaining process in the course of which each failed attempt to restore the loss results in its own mini reaction of perhaps further pain. So it is easy to see how multiple losses may result in a bewildering emotional state.

The fog of emotional overload and burn-out

After a while it becomes impossible to make any sense of the feelings being experienced in such a situation. Life has developed into a chaos so appalling that all one can do is merely to get through each day. The survival response is simply to switch off emotionally and run on in an automatic numbness. This is not denial, and it is not depression. It is emotional overload.

This is the state in which many people arrive in the surgery. As a consequence of their emotional overload their lives are heading for some sort of a breakdown, either at work or in their marriage, or in their friendships or community. It is extremely difficult to penetrate the emotional fog and make any sense of life. They question whether they are suffering from an illness. Physical illness is known to arise more commonly during bereavement than at other times – possibly because the stressed hormone balance of the body, when pushed to an extreme, somehow hinders the activity of the immune system. For this reason it may be important for a doctor to make a medical examination and arrange some basic tests to exclude the possibility of illness. However, this is not always necessary, and it would be wrong to medicalize grief. Grief itself is not an illness.

The role of unrecognzed grief in ME (or chronic fatigue syndrome)

It is not yet proven, but I have a strong suspicion that the condition known as ME (myalgic encephalomyelitis) or, as doctors prefer to call it, chronic fatigue syndrome (CFS), may in part be caused by unrecognized and unresolved loss reactions. As we have already said, we know that recognized grief makes physical illness more common, so it is quite probable that unrecognized grief could be doing something similar to weaken the immune system.

I remember a woman in her early thirties who was developing chronic fatigue with joint pains. Some blood tests had suggested she might have a very early inflammatory disease like rheumatoid arthritis, but others did not fit with this diagnosis. Something unusual was going on. Her mood and energy were low, but there was no obvious depression in a medical sense. There were no family or work problems to account for her sense of malaise. When talking around the background it emerged that her father had died when she was only fifteen years old. She told me what a marvellous man he had been, and it began to appear that she had never grieved properly because during the difficult first week after he died she had wanted to be the strong one for the rest of the family. She had not attended the funeral, nor properly said goodbye to him, and now was also full of regrets that he had not been around in her later teens when she could have got to know him better. She was suffering from unresolved grief. We started to talk about grief, and fortunately the family attended a supportive church where prayer-counselling was available. Over several months she worked through her emotions of grief openly with the family and pastor and counsellor and doctor. Her condition improved, and, remarkably, the blood test also reverted to normal.

Most doctors believe that ME is caused by some factor delaying recovery from an otherwise short-lived illness, such as a viral infection, thereby making it self-perpetuating. Many of us have experienced times when the body feels weak and when every action requires a deliberate effort, but most of us recover from this after a brief period. But if the recovery of a previously fit person's recovery from a simple illness is delayed, their natural feelings of loss are increased by many extra losses of normal activity and expectations. This might trap the body's chemistry in an unhelpful spiral of inactivity and draining of energy as every attempt to find a way out fails. 'Why aren't I getting any better? There must be something seriously wrong with me!'

Some researchers using questionnaires designed to detect depression have found it to be commonly associated with ME, so doctors will often say that ME is a type of depression. But I think this badly misses the point. If one of the common factors is a restricted immune response caused by grief, then it becomes easy to see how a vicious cycle of loss and illness can rapidly build up when an illness does not resolve. There will be loss of well-being, loss of activity, loss of social contacts, loss of progress at work, loss of self-respect, loss of plans, loss of hope. This spiralling complex loss reaction could affect the immune system in a way that makes any progress to recovery even more difficult. Although the depressive phase of grief may be detectable by a questionnaire, it would be particularly unhelpful do describe this as a depressive illness, because to do so adds stigma and a fear of loss of one's sanity to all the other losses, plus a sense of injustice that can bring an unhelpful anger-guilt whirlpool to our emotions. I have certainly found it worth exploring the losses that sufferers of this condition feel, and this may help to speed the recovery that usually does occur over many months of planned rests, interspersed with graded exercise that restore confidence and fitness.

Thus ME may be partly a complex loss reaction present in a culture that has forgotten that we do grieve. Most people with multiple losses do not, however, come to the surgery suffering from ME, or thinking that they may be suffering from it. Tiredness is usually a feature of complex loss reactions, but there are as many varieties of reported symptoms as there are people. Each of us is unique in this. What we do all need, however, is a structured approach which helps us to understand how to deal with not knowing what we feel.

Using the worksheet to see through emotional overload

If you want to get inside your emotional switch-off caused by overload then you must, repeat *must*, be willing to give time to it. The worksheet shown in Figure 1 has been used with great success with many patients. It is designed to help you structure that period of overload so that it becomes time usefully spent and not just frittered away.

NAMED LOSSES	SHOCK	DENIAL	ANGER	GUILT	BARG'N	DEPR'N	ACCEPT
JOB			✓				
MONEY	✓						
SELF RESPECT				✓			

Figure 1

The first thing to do is to get hold of your own sheet of paper, preferably about A4 size, or you may prefer to use the inside of an old breakfast cereal box. Rule on the vertical lines in roughly the positions shown. Then along the top of the worksheet copy the seven stages of loss reactions. You will find it helpful to have understood these seven stages first by reading chapters one and two before attempting to use the worksheet! ('If all else fails, read the instructions.' – this classic piece of advice was written for people on automatic pilot.)

Down the left hand edge of the sheet there should be a wide column headed 'LOSSES' at the top. To use this column, find a place and a time when you can be alone. Then, in

safety, think back over your life to identify as many significant losses as you can – ones that were important to you at
the time. Those in the last year or two will probably come to
mind fairly quickly, but there will be others from earlier
years, and even your childhood, which still cause hurt when
we think back over them. For example, you might write
something about how your brother repeatedly insulted you,
or how all those years ago your best friend left you when
you were already feeling lonely. Such memories may still
arouse strong emotion, and this emotion arising from unaccepted loss can even now be affecting how you handle your
present losses.

Include in this list the 'What ifs . . .' of your life, and the 'If
onlys . . .' (You are bound to start going over these hypo-
thetical situations in your mind as you read this, but you
will find there is a very real advantage in actually writing
them down on your own sheet.)

Be as specific as possible. Loss of mother, for instance,
may include several different aspects that each hurt if you
think about them. Mother may have been a companion to
talk to, and someone who gave a sense of order to life, and a
root into the family history. Each of these may bring grief
that is worked through to acceptance at a different pace as
we eventually bargain our way through to adjustments *for
that particular aspect of life that mother represents for us*.
So under the heading 'Mother' you might risk writing some
sub-headings such as 'loss of companionship', 'loss of
orderliness', 'loss of roots'. Even those aspects about
mother that irritated you can bring their own grief as we
lose the familiarity of life.

You will probably quickly discover that finding the
words to name your feelings *as losses* does not come naturally to you. We tend to cover up our hurts by phrasing
things in a roundabout way. For example, rather than saying I have 'lost a sense that there is justice in the world' we

tend to talk about 'our sense of powerlessness to do anything about the injustices of the world'. To avoid this feature of our humanity we need to spend a moment reflecting on, 'Just what *is* the loss underlying this bad feeling I have?', and then name it as a definite loss.

The idea of this list is to write a series of headings and sub-headings only on the worksheet itself. Many people, once they allow themselves to start thinking like this, need to write at greater length to express the pent-up emotions of years ago. They may fill several sheets of paper, and that is often all to the good. Having discovered the depth and breadth of those emotions, each loss still needs to be given a heading or sub-heading, and that title written on the worksheet.

Having identified and named the losses, either then, or on another occasion, start to spend a few moments reflecting on each one in turn. For this second part of the exercise it is important to be able to run down the whole list in one sitting, but not to rush through any of the individual losses. As you spend a few moments contemplating each loss in turn, ask yourself, 'Right at this moment, what do I feel about this particular loss?' Names of feelings may elude you, or you may feel flooded by names, but try to decide which of the seven stages they relate to, and place a tick (preferably using a pencil) in the relevant column for that loss. The scatter of ticks that you see on the page gives you a useful insight into the very centre of your soul. The reason it is best to use a pencil is that if you were to repeat the exercise a week later, the scatter of ticks would be different, because the losses are being processed. It may for a moment be useful to compare one array of ticks with another, but if we cherish the pattern of ticks we had a week ago more than our present state of heart, then perhaps there is a problem of letting go which will need to be addressed. Rubbing out last weeks pattern of ticks could be quite symbolic if it is done at the beginning of another time of reflection. It is like getting an occasional photograph of your inner emotional life. These 'reconnaissance photographs' can help you to see through your emotional overload and plan what next to focus your mind upon in the depths of your heart.

I remember one woman who, several years after adopting a child, still recorded a sense of shock that she could not have her own children. Her inner life was full with other losses which began to be processed as we started to use this complex loss reaction analysis, but this one remained in shock. It was a valuable insight to gain. She began to realize how much effect this was having in her life, and what a demand her way of coping with this was putting upon other people she closely related to. Rather than focusing upon all the minor losses that followed as a consequence of the way she was behaving, she began to look again at her resources for adjusting to life as it really was. No longer nursing an 'if only . . .', life began to improve. It did not become 'all sweetness and light', but everything came into perspective and she discovered how despite disappointments she could get on with being creative.

When thinking about a particular loss as you slowly run your finger down your list, you may find that several emotions arise, such as anger, guilt and depression all mixed up. If this happens, then you are probably bargaining hard to restore that loss and the tick should go in the 'bargaining' column. This is because bargaining can be a very prolonged phase. If we are yearning or longing to restore what we have lost, then every time we realize we are failing to restore it we experience another mini loss reaction for that aspect we were trying to restore, and this new reaction brings its own anger, guilt and powerlessness.

Having ticked the 'bargaining' column, it may be worth trying to identify if there are different aspects of the loss you are trying to restore, and separate those out as separate headings in your list. Likewise, if you think you have truly accepted a certain loss, but there is a slight twinge of anger or guilt still about it, then the way to handle this is to try to break the heading of your loss down into smaller sections. Then, try to see which of those aspects you have truly accepted, and which you are denying. You may discover that each emotion you can identify relates to a totally different aspect, which the loss you have named only *represents*. For example, somebody who had been abused in childhood made a list which included loss of her pet dog. She felt angry, sad and afraid when she thought of this. We managed to clarify that the *anger* related to the fact that she had nursed the dog from an abandoned state into health only for him then to die of cancer, about which she felt a sense of injustice in the world. The *sadness* arose from true acceptance of the loss of comfort from her play-mate, which she had bargained through by buying another puppy. Her *fear* arose because this loss represented her inability to prevent the intrusion of something unpleasant into her life so that she doubted her resources to create a place of safety. So when she made out a new list, under 'loss of pet dog' appeared three sub-headings, 'a sense of justice', 'comfort in playfulness' and 'ability to prevent intrusion', all of which gave significant insights into the other losses in her life.

The third stage of using this worksheet is to leave it behind. After a while the names of the seven stages of the loss reactions will be well known to you. Then, whenever and wherever you find yourself thinking about any of your losses, you will have this framework in the back of your mind to help make sense of it all.

Using the worksheet for relationship difficulties

Although nowadays the brokenness of many families is open knowledge, whereas it used to be a concealed secret, there is nevertheless such a deep mystery in the permanence of marriage that people still long to commit themselves to it, even time and again! We can all spend a lifetime contemplating what this says about human nature and still learn something new from the unity between people that can be experienced in a family. Similar bondings occur in friendships, with adoptions, and between unmarried partners. These strong relationships help us to make sense of life, but they are usually most stable if there is a permanent and enduring marriage somewhere in the background of the experience of those who are in the relationship.

When times are difficult, communication with those who are close to us can become very poor. Being in a state of emotional overload not only robs us of insight into our own hearts, but also makes it very difficult for others to make accurate guesses about what is going on inside us. When we are withdrawn, we may not realize that someone close to us will themselves feel that as *their* loss. Our spouse or friend or partner will have to start processing their own loss reaction because there is something about us that they have lost. Some will be better at this than others. If for any reason they are not very good at it, then an unhappy interaction begins – a sort of carousel, as one projects their loss reaction emotions onto the other and back again. This is why the complex loss reaction analysis sheet can be so useful in relationship difficulties.

All friendships have occasional rough patches, but solutions to problems may start to appear when you begin to analyse the other's behaviour in terms of complex losses. What for your friend represents a loss? Ask him or her! And if there is any hesitation to state it, then write out two complex loss analysis sheets and let each of you complete one. It may bring the focus needed for both of you. It may be best that you both complete them separately first of all, but every couple will be different again in this. Even if one refuses to do it, the very fact of mentioning losses will alter the conversation between you. And once the multiple losses are down on paper, amazing things can start to happen in the midst of a seemingly hopeless situation.

How does this come about? Often a serious cause of difficulty in a relationship is that when one person is emotionally 'prickly' about something and the other does not know why, the other starts to make guesses. These may be wildly mistaken, in which case they are likely to produce unhelpful responses. This is especially likely when there are multiple losses and the sufferer does not know what he or she is feeling. Using these analysis sheets, however, means that when one person names a particular loss, perhaps even points to it on the page, and talks about the emotional stage being felt, the other is not only able to empathise with the feelings being described, but is also able to know which memories are generating the emotion at that time. The emotion can then be seen to come not because of some failure of the partner to please the other, but from specific memories that need healing.

The value of both partners writing things down goes beyond even being able to understand the reasons for the reactions of the other. To know somebody is more than being in possession of certain information about them. Knowing someone involves sticking around long enough to feel moved by their emotions. When your partner uses the worksheet in this way, you may feel their emotions of anger or guilt about the relevant loss, but they also feel your presence, in addition to any pain. That is when they begin to know healing.

Preventing further relationship problems by using loss analysis

Within a relationship where people feel a bond every prospect of change carries the hope of gain and the risk of loss.

To deny the losses involved in change will inevitably cause problems later at some level or another in the relationship. Failing to count the cost of that change for each other will eventually result in the emotions of loss creeping up on us from behind when we least expect it! Arguments, chilliness, the chance affair that seems a more attractive bargain . . . How can we prevent this happening?

The more we encourage and train ourselves to think about our losses without shame and come to see them as a normal part of a full life, the more we shall be able to notice and understand the ways others tend to react to loss. We are then in the position where, if we choose, we can prevent problems developing in relationships generally. The loss reaction analysis assists this process by giving us a useful 'tool' – a simple, shared language with our partners or friends in which we agree the words mean the same thing. Thus, when we tell our friends or partners that we are feeling angry or guilty or depressed about any particular incident or change, these terms will be understood not as meaning 'this needs criticism or judgement about wrongdoing'. Rather they will realize that 'there is a loss reaction going on'. They will help us to try to identify and name this loss so that we can better count the cost of changing together.

That is when we begin to know the depths of true freedom.

CHAPTER 4

Obsessional Disorders of Eating or of Other Behaviour

Drives and obsessions

Do you know anybody who repeatedly does something, like tidying the room the instant it becomes untidy, when nobody else is taking it so seriously. Do you yourself tend to behave in this way, possibly surprising your family and friends? You don't know why you do whatever it may be, but you know that you would feel uncomfortable if you did not. It seems as if you need to do it even though it may consume a lot of your time and energy and prevent you from doing other things. Is there any explanation for this behaviour?

In the previous chapter we started to look at how our emotions and relationships can become complicated if several losses happen together in a fairly short period of time. In this chapter and the next two we shall look at how each person's own unique personality can add extra features to this complication. Many of these unique facets of our personalities become noticeable only when we are secretly anticipating losses. It is important to emphasize that we must not become self-critical as we grow to recognize them. They are part of the complex marvel of life. We all share humanity and no two human beings are the same.

All of us sometimes feel a strong drive to act in some particular way. Usually we can choose to withstand the impulse ('I feel I want to scream out!'), and others will never know that we have resisted such a drive. We resist these drives because we have reason to believe that acting on them would in some way harm us or others whom we care about. But imagine what would happen if we believed that obeying the drive would make us, or others, more secure. It's very likely that we would do the thing with a conviction that what we were doing was right. This is the basis of the obsessions that so commonly affect human behaviour.

Obsessions are sometimes confused with phobias. But they are not the same at all. Phobias are drives *to avoid* something seen to be *negative*. Obsessions, by contrast, are drives *towards something* seen to be *positive*. Obsessional behaviour is much more common than people realize. Most of us, for example, demonstrate the potential for obsessional thinking on those occasions when a tune goes round and round in our heads. In an average suburban street about one house in twenty will be home to a person who actually has a problem because obsessional thinking has started to noticeably affect their behaviour, and one house in sixty will be home to somebody quite disabled by their obsession.

Giving in to drives only becomes a medical problem when it happens so repeatedly and frequently that it disorders our ability to run our life on a daily basis. Taking a long shower at least five times a day is not only expensive, but also restrictive both for the person concerned and for the rest of the household. Behaviour that disrupts our daily life is called an obsessional disorder. However, an obsessional disorder is only an extreme of a normal human behaviour.

Nearly everybody affected by obsessional behaviour fears that others will think they are stupid. To avoid shame they keep it secret even from their doctors. But obsessional behaviour is not a sign of incapacity. It is only an outward sign of a unfulfilled desire that we all share – a basic need to feel secure. Obsessional behaviour is what I call a fringe behaviour. Just as waves breaking on the shore, on the fringes of an ocean, may tell us there has been a storm far out at sea, so an obsessional drive breaking out into behaviour tells us there is turmoil in our inner heart, a storm in which we fear we may drown if we head into it.

Obsessions can disorder our lives in various ways. Some people need to go round inspecting the locks repeatedly, or checking the electric sockets or gas taps; others constantly confirm that the soap is placed just right by the sink, or clean the house so that it is spotless; others may wash their hands a certain number of times, or may frequently check that their body tissue is not wasting away. Very commonly people become obsessed about food. Here there are two extremes: some are anorexic and lose weight because they refuse to eat, others, who are bulimic, gain weight because they binge eat and then make themselves sick. Anorexia and bulimia can go together.

The distress associated with these disordering drives can be considerable, and the underlying reasons why they have become out of control may be completely unknown. But even if the reason is known, even if the storm has been identified and is known to have blown itself out, that alone does not stop the behaviour. What is going on?

Obsessional disorder and the need to control the world out there

Basically, obsessional behaviour arises when people try to control the risk of loss by attempting to control the world 'out there'.

I can remember a teenager who had started to develop bulimia. She and her parents could not identify a cause until we started to do a loss reaction analysis. Then working over a few weeks with the girl on her own it became clear that the loss of a boyfriend some time previously had affected her quite deeply. In addition to this, comments from other people had made her blame her body shape. Her diet was entirely reasonable. The bulimic behaviour, however, occurred only when any other young man expressed an interest in her. Then the fear of losing him, even before she had gained him, drove her into this anticipatory loss reaction with its extreme bargaining gambit. The insight into this pattern finally calmed her 'storm out at sea'. The problem behaviour did stop, and she started a new relationship.

Sometimes we are so overwhelmed by confused and threatening emotions inside us that we feel our inner world has passed completely beyond our control. We may be unable to identify or name the most significant losses while still anticipating further losses. Obsessional behaviour as some sort of a structure may persist, even though the cause of the initial storm has gone, until other methods of 'bargaining' for the hidden losses can be developed. Until then we may thrash around looking for stability and security but are unable to find it. So we may be driven to assert ourselves again and again in the outside world and establish some control out there because we fear drowning in the chaos within. Although we cannot control our inner turmoil, we can hope to find something or someone in the outer world that will yield to our need to establish structure, and so feed a fleeting sense of security. We may feel we are the victim of circumstances and of our emotions, but we will find someone or something that we can control.

Truly ordering the world around us is bound to involve times of conflict with others. Some assertive people can handle this; but respectful assertion can become aggressive bullying when an insecure individual feels in danger of being overwhelmed by an anticipated loss, and thus compelled to fight to win at all costs. Too much depends on it to lose. The person who feels that everything depends on victory, and who dare not lose, will often leave behind a trail of hurt people. Hurt – but also bewildered. Why has something comparatively trivial (such as whether to have smoked or unsmoked ham in the sandwiches after a funeral) generated so much heat? This method of finding security by anger may work for a while until the person with the obsession loses a battle – and then insecurity sets in.

Other assertive people who need to control the world 'out there' choose to avoid that conflict. Instead they try to control some aspect of their own behaviour in the world; this is a battle they know they can win. Controlling their food intake is one way, controlling the locks on doors is another, and so on. For people who have been emotionally, physically, or sexually abused or hurt, controlling locks or chocolates offers the possibility of ensuring that a glimmer of self-respect will survive.

By no means all people with obsessive behaviour have been abused in any way. The problem experienced by some is that they feel the standards set to please the people they love are so high that they have no reasonable hope of being able to reach them. They may feel they have lost the love they value even before they start trying. For them, an obsession is an attempt to show they can at least reach some standard set for themselves. ('I can never give her what she wants, but I can at least achieve something by ensuring that I have the cleanest car in the road.')

One might think that the way ahead in these situations would be to give up the obsessional behaviour. But doing this could mean that the overwhelmed or the discouraged person might lose that last glimmer of self-respect and hope. Surrendering one's self respect is a very risky thing to do. It makes sense only when something else is happening that supplies greater self-respect and security. Such a discovery is an important part of healing from obsessional behaviour. Greater self-respect comes automatically, like maturity, as we begin to clearly recognize and name the significant areas of loss in our lives, and complete the grief. It is after fully accepting our powerlessness over some areas of life, while recognizing our skills to name and restore *what the loss might represent*, that we can *become* aware of our creativity in other areas of life. Then we can reasonably hope to know the forgiveness – and experience the surrender – that is safe when we trust in the love of others. The process is summed up well in that famous 'Serenity Prayer':

> Please grant me the serenity to accept the things I cannot change,
> The courage to change the things I can change,
> And the wisdom to know the difference.

Anger and guilt as a trap like a whirlpool

Underlying obsessional behaviour can be a vicious cycle of *anger* and *guilt*. This cycle becomes a trap, rather like a whirlpool. *Anger* expresses itself in that assertive drive to control the world out there, but following the resulting driven behaviour (such as over-eating or constant washing), there comes a wave of *guilt*. Here lies the clue that hidden loss reactions are at work.

The danger arises from this type of hidden loss reaction when we begin to believe the feeling of guilt means the assertive drive they are experiencing has been caused by their having done something wrong, either in the past, or more recently. Now we can see why is important to name the secret underlying loss, since the obsessive drive is not the result of wrong behaviour but a 'bargaining' attempt to restore that loss. When a bargain fails, as obsessive behaviour always does, there is another mini-loss reaction with anger and guilt. The guilt is like an unavoidable stepping stone where we are compelled to pause and question what our role has been in creating that loss. For obsessive people the feeling of guilt that is associated with this questioning may be deepened by regrets at having felt angry towards the ones they love, and by self-doubt about whether they are safe in being angry towards the ones they fear. The whirlpool begins to spin when the guilt is followed by a sense of injustice (because they *know* they have not done anything wrong or unreasonable)! This sense of outrage brings a return to anger, and with the anger there is once more a drive to control whatever is controllable again.

The whole cycle of anger and guilt can force people into lower and lower self-respect because they cannot identify what they 'clearly must' – as they think – have done wrong, and especially so if, as a part of abuse, someone has been repeatedly told they were at fault so that they also doubt their own judgement. Nobody has ever told them instead that all this anguish and tumult could arise simply because they feel they have lost something important. If they knew that, rather than keep it secret or shrouded in shame, they could be allowed to name the loss and grieve openly about it right through to true acceptance or to successful bargaining to restore it, then the whirlpool would become shallower and shallower. Eventually the ceaseless spinning round and round and down and down would stop; the whirlpool would become only a ripple in the memory as the ensuing mixture of sadness and joy would be acknowledged and shared with trusted loved ones.

Moving on from feelings of guilt

Moving on from guilt can be a problem, however. If we cannot move on from guilt, then we cannot bargain effectively, nor accept our losses.

Guilt is an irrational emotion that has its own emotional logic. Guilt does not respond to reason. It does not disappear when presented with evidence that there is no truth in it. This feeling of guilt is in effect a question. But we all know that an answer to a question often only breeds more questions. Friends and relatives who try to reassure someone about their doubts may well find all they achieve is to create distrust and doubt concerning themselves rather than the radiant confidence they hoped for. They themselves may despair as all their attempts at reassurance fail in the face of persistent guilt. It is almost as if the loss reaction is being forced onto those around. Here is another reason for looking at the link between guilt and punishment: if there is a problem about moving on from guilt, the persistent guilt has the effect of punishing others.

When they are overwhelmed by guilt, people usually feel they ought to be punished – 'It's my fault. She wouldn't be dead now if I had taken more care.' But what is this punishment? Punishment is the process and feelings that come, driven by an anger that may be creatively controlled or destructively uncontrolled, as the hurt that has arisen from previous loss of right relationship is made public or open. It is important to see that punishment *is not in itself* a legal balancing of the accounts. It is not the same as revenge or retribution, nor even in itself correction for fault, because it can be directed equally at oneself or someone else held responsible for the loss. On the contrary, true punishment *is* the means we have of fulfilling our psychological need for openness in relationships about loss. It cannot be a pleasant process, letting our losses out into the light in the fearful hope that we shall find greater security as a result, so no wonder sometimes we avoid it and let our loss reactions fester instead in dark hibernation, hiding from (or occasionally striking at) whoever might disturb them.

In this context, 'mercy' or 'being merciful' means being sensitive enough to hear about the hurt even though listening may be a punishing experience. If we are merciful, we are all punished by news of loss. We each can make different sorts of responses to this 'punishment' we receive by listening to the loss-sufferer who is taking a risk to share their guilty feelings, and our responses may be more, or less, helpful. We can respond with apathy, mockery, self-defence, or with sympathy, empathy, and with measures to bring redress for loss or containment of a cause of the loss which may be lenient or severe, and so on. These measures to bring redress are often *called* punishment if a human perpetrator can be identified, but in fact courts of law apply *penalties* as an optional *part* of true punishment. The penalties only bring about punishment if the perpetrator is moved towards restoring right and open relationships. Otherwise the penalties can be shrugged off by some heartless perpetrators; or, alternatively, a guilt-ridden loss-sufferer might subject themselves to endless penalties in the hope of bringing about true *punishment*.

Put in these terms, the role of punishment is to move grief along. However, when we are already grieving, it is that later stage of powerlessness that springs the trap of persisting guilty feelings. Can we come to terms with our own powerlessness in these situations without falling into the role of being an eternal victim instead of simply a human being getting to know our limits like everybody else? If not, then guilty feelings will remain. When we are faced with a person plagued by persistent guilt, or if you recognize some of this in the depths of your own heart, it is more helpful to explore the problems of coming to terms with powerlessness than to start reasoning either about how they, or you, were not at fault, or about how to punish or apply penalties to oneself or others.

The solution to guilt is not just punishment. Punishment is a step on the way to forgiveness, and forgiveness is the solution to guilty feelings. I would go so far as to say that there is no other solution to guilty feelings than forgiveness. There is no pill known to doctors that works against guilty feelings and no counselling can, in itself, evaporate the anger of loss which drives punishment. However, the good news is that as we explore the limitations of our powerlessness and the apparent powerfulness of others, then we might gradually allow ourselves to forgive and find the way to break through into creativity again. More will be said about powerlessness, and the bargaining that is relevant to it, in Chapter 7.

Forgiveness is, in fact, taking that giant leap from anger straight through to acceptance of loss. We shall look at this more closely in Chapter 6, but it is worth saying here that this explains why forgiveness is often so difficult, because packed inside forgiveness is fear, doubt, anger, guilt, yearning, despair. Of course it is risky! This whole method of analysing our loss reactions, which includes moving on from guilty feelings, is effectively a way of stretching out forgiveness of ourselves and of others into manageable small risks.

If persistent guilty feelings trouble you, then possibly 'loss of openness' should be on your analysis list – with a tick in the 'denial' column.

The importance of loss of trust in childhood

There is one final aspect of loss analysis that is important to mention in relation to obsessional disorders. Often what underlies obsessional behaviours is some kind of loss experienced in childhood or adolescence. Typically, the loss of friends through a family move, or the sudden loss of a parent through abandonment or death, can cause children to have a strong desire to control the world out there, and at the same time to doubt their ability to do so. The timing of these losses, during childhood, can add another type of low self-respect which complicates development into adult maturity.

When our childhood losses hibernate, they trap normal emotional development. Our emotional development in respect of one particular aspect of our lives is stopped at the stage of life we were in when the loss occurred. Thus somebody who was as a child falsely accused of some wrongdoing, but was afraid to speak out about it, might find that in adult life the threat of false accusation might trigger a memory of the child-like powerlessness which was present at the time of the original loss. This might prevent them from making a reasonable adult response to the present situation, even though in other areas of life they might be relating well to others and functioning from a position of normal adult self-assurance. Even though all the other aspects of our life may mature in the normal way, unresolved losses are like snags that can catch us and hold us back. When this happens, these areas of our lives prompt an emotional response whose strength reflects our childhood feelings when the loss first occurred. The emotion may be shock or fear, denial, anger, guilt, self-justification, or powerless passivity; whatever the type of feeling, it is likely to be out of proportion to the present circumstances.

Mature behaviour is not about independence, but inter-dependence. We mature from the dependency upon people more powerful than ourselves into adult-adult right relationships between people who know we differ from each other but who equally recognize the value of the differences between us. In mature inter-dependence we experience freedom to be ourselves, while contributing ourselves to the identity of others. But when we suddenly face our unresolved loss, things change. It is this element of equal contribution that becomes frightening. We are reminded of the impossibility of achieving inter-dependence with the people who had caused our sense of loss at a time when we were dependent upon them, and this reminder can send people into a downward spiral of poor self-respect.

The difficulty about childhood and adolescent losses is that, in order to grow in self-respect so as to make a right adult-adult relationship with those who have caused your loss, it may seem necessary to walk a path of independence for a while. Independence means feeling able to do whatever you choose without reference to another person. In such a relationship there is no responsiveness, no contributing to each other's identity, and effectively no relationship. Such independence may serve as a safe bolt-hole, but it is also a trap in which people have no hope of love or admiration. Happily, the walk into independence need only be a temporary expedition before experiments with mature inter-dependence can be re-started.

Such experiments are part of adolescent growing up, risky but necessary sometimes. It is less often recognized that even for adults, within a marriage, the snags remain in certain specific areas of our emotional development. There is likely to be trouble if one partner strikes out for independence from the other in order to sort out one particular area. That is where marriage vows can be helpful: 'for better, for worse'. They assist a couple to pass through a difficult time of this nature on their path to overall maturity by helping each other to 'unsnag' from the past.

Two things are vital when the time comes to start working through these loss reactions, either within a long-term relationship or before settling with a life partner. The first is to learn how to honestly name your feelings to each other. Then, if the emotion is in the loss reaction sequence, learn how to help each other go on to name the losses which underlie those feelings. There is a cultural taboo against talking about our feelings of loss, and I have found that many people are quite tongue-tied when it comes to naming these feelings. That is why Chapter 9 contains seven lists of words that name the range of feelings which can fall within each of the loss reaction stages. The lists are not exhaustive, but they give an idea of the breadth of feeling 'ordinary' people may experience, even if the feelings remain un-named! (At this point readers may wish to glance ahead into the chapter *Finding Time and Finding Words* to scan the lists relevant to Anger and Guilt.)

If you have been completing a complex loss analysis sheet and have a tendency to obsessional behaviour, you may find that this arises from anticipating that the problems which arose in your childhood are going to be repeated in your present main relationships. If so, then you may well need to add, at the bottom of your list, 'loss of trust'.

CHAPTER 5

Dependencies on Others

Failing to recognize how much others do to create our environment

An important part of being a parent is making an environment that nurtures others. Although children may generally not be able to say what they expect from their parents, they do know when their expectations are not met. That is what they call 'unfair'. As we mature we move from child-like dependency on parental figures who create our environment into adulthood, where we learn to create our own environment in balance with others. We may then develop further to a parental role in which we create an environment that is principally nurturing for others. Single people often develop nurturing roles through caring for others in the family or in society. We even eventually move through this into a fully mature state where we can flexibly move between all three of these roles as is appropriate for any given time. We learn how to both receive support and give help.

There is another important feature of this four-stage picture of maturation which is sometimes missed. It is easy to become dependent on some nurturing environment without realizing that we are, in fact, dependent on the *people* who are quietly creating it. We value this kind of nurturing environment especially after a sudden loss. At such a time we are glad to be given extra special attention – the phone calls, the cooked meals, the offers of help. But unless we have already come to understand the nature of a nurturing environment in less extreme situations, then we have been living within a potential trap, and if this trap closes it might seriously delay our growing up.

Imagine for a moment that we have failed to realize how much personal work and effort has gone into making and sustaining a caring and nurturing environment. We haven't understood how many people have put effort into providing material comfort, and emotional and spiritual stability and support. If we are in this state of ignorance, then when people seem to fail us by not doing the right things to keep our environment comfortable, we may be caught in a complicated set of loss reactions. Individuals react in various ways to this type of loss; but one common feature is likely to recur. We will all try to force other people into patterns of behaviour to secure, above everything else, the nurturing environment we long for.

This may be what is going on when people complain: 'I felt let down by the family/ the church/ the organisation/ the club!' Underlying this is the cry: 'In my time of need you failed to nurture me in the way I wanted. I deserve better than this.' In the face of loss, we will demand our rights, even if we have none, because we feel we are being unfairly treated. In this situation the quality of our environment has become more important to us than the quality of our relationship with the other people who are sharing it and sustaining it.

Somebody caught in this trap may be suffering from a variety of losses. Trying to analyse them in order to bring comfort can be quite complicated. Rather often it may seem as if this person's life does not contain much loss. After all, so long as others do what we want, we feel that we're winning. But the losses are there, and when, sooner or later, they are recognized, the experience may be profoundly disturbing. The reason is that most of these losses have been blocked in the shock stage. The shock emerges as fear as soon as we contemplate the loss of our comfort.

If this fear is tinged with anger, it will likely be expressed in the kind of dependent relationship of somebody who, while arrogantly ruling and bossing people, is dependent upon having people around who can be bossed. This person is trying to maintain the comfort and quell the fear by convincing ourselves that they are in control. If, on the other hand, this fear is tinged with guilt, the dependent relationship is different; we see somebody who by remaining passive and seemingly weak manipulates others into nurturing them, and who is dependent upon having people around who are motivated to create a comfortable environment for the 'sufferer' because he or she seems to be in need. Both types of dependency produce the same result: the person concerned maintains the comfort and quells the fear by convincing themselves that they are safe.

Sometimes we see this latter dependency in people recovering from a mental breakdown. For example, a married woman who is being cared for in this situation by her husband may feel excessive guilt at the pressure being caused to her partner by the extra burden of work. Facing that guilt may be very painful. But by becoming even more dependent and demanding she may succeed in using the nurturing environment as a drug to soften this pain. Differently – but similarly involving an attempt to gain control – a husband who is trying to cope with his own sense of loss (caused by the illness of his partner) may feel excessive anger. This may result in his becoming very bossy, and as his wife is around, she feels much of the force of that desire to control. The two become locked in a critical-parent/manipulating-child relationship.

Fear is a loss reaction blocked at the stage of shock

It is shock that causes the mental and emotional paralysis which makes dependency a trap and which results in our seeking comfort rather than face reality. Shock prevents us from getting anywhere close to accepting the basic truth that maturing must involve loss. It seems impossible that this should be true when those who maturely create our environment seem so much stronger than we are. If something goes wrong we automatically push them to put it right, rather than accept that things will never be quite the same again. But accepting this loss must precede the realization that nevertheless we might actually be able to 'run with' that and survive, and even thrive! At any and every stage in our lives we are likely to find ourselves hoping that we may gain something more by simply staying where we are. However, being fully alive brings with it a sense that we need to be making progress. Even when we have realized this, though, it is sometimes difficult to accept that we progress to other stages in life only as we come to terms with our limitations in each earlier stage.

To imagine that we might mature without obvious gain might strike some as odd.

Some people make the mistake of trying to mature by 'stealing' a gain. They rob the fruits of a later stage of life without first giving up their ways of an earlier stage, which is in effect a false growing up. Pre-marital sex is one example: a couple may want the gain of a sexual relationship but yet be afraid of losing independence. In terms of loss and gain, the problem with making this choice is that when a couple do later marry, they will find they have much more to give up, in order to create a true 'home' than they previously realized. The 'shocking' losses of maturation have been denied, but only for a time. They will re-emerge at some point and possibly cause trouble for the marriage.

If we are to succeed in bargaining through the losses involved in moving from one stage of life to another we shall need emotional stability. But how can we expect to develop emotional stability through the tumult of loss reactions involved if we have never had role models of strong adult or parent figures whom we can admire and respect and love? There are very many people in this situation. It is, after all, not in any way their fault. So once they notice that others have had something different in their upbringing, they may be burdened with a sense of unfairness. This, of course, is itself not the most stable emotional base to work from. For somebody in this position the losses involved in maturation can be extremely threatening. The sense that something is lacking from their lives can bring a feeling of panic. Although people may want to leave painful parts of their lives behind, they find, in what seems a contradiction, that they are unable to do so. Doing so would mean losing what little there is for them to hang onto. ('I may not have had a happy childhood, but I seem unable to leave home. At least home is familiar. I can't imagine myself living a normal life without being here.') People can have a deep doubt that they are able to meet the requirements of some new role for themselves. If they feel unable to 'bargain on' from here then they may become dependent upon even the most imperfect of environments and people.

There are several temporary solutions to this problem and to delay the time when we lose the nurture of having someone else create our environment. Friendships can turn into self-supporting cliques. A clique can turn into a cult. Any kind of cult, be it religious or political, can develop when an angry-dependant individual teams up with a number of guilty-dependants. The latter may genuinely want to improve themselves, but are too shocked to bargain their way in the wider world. Instead, they gather around the one who seems strong. If only there had been strong role models around for them when, as adolescents, they were going through a critical stage in their lives. Parents apart, it might have been an uncle and aunt or a godparent who would go on taking an interest, being there as somebody 'outside' to emulate.

Other comfort substitutes may be found. Young people may marry in passion and never realize that they have not understood what mature love is as they then expect their partner to be a substitute parent as well as wife or husband. Shock may prevent a man from realizing until it is too late that manly love involves self-sacrifice if the wife and home are to thrive. All goes well until a baby is born. The wife is unable to nurture her man as well as her baby. How does a young man react then?

When loss produces a shock/fear reaction some women look for comfort substitutes in their children. It is obviously fair for a child to be dependant on parental figures for nurturing, but not fair when a parental figure is dependant upon the child for her nurturing. If one's identity as a mother is dependent upon a child being within a certain age range, then some sort of relationship problem is bound to develop as the mother experiences difficulty in letting her child grow up and grow away. At this point a good husband will be able to help her through her loss adjustment, while encouraging maturity in the younger members of the family.

Knowing when to let go is so difficult. The marriage ceremony used to be important as a 'letting-go', a ritual severing of the bond between parents and child whom the parents had seen mature from a baby to their adult son or daughter. Sadly, it seldom happens like that. Parents fail their offspring by not letting go at this stage, with the result that the unaccepted loss may turn a caring mother into the most damaging sort of mother-in-law. People say, 'Don't think of yourself as losing a daughter, but as gaining a son!' It may sound like comforting wisdom, but it is denial at its worst, and trouble will follow unless the loss of the daughter (or son!) is accepted as well.

We all have to guess our own way through these various dependencies when the time comes for the next stage. Multiple loss analysis can be helpful at any of these transitional stages in life as we move from one role to another. But most of us have difficulty in finding sufficient private time to make an honest assessment of our situation and evaluate what it is that we are losing at each stage. Remember, there is no need to show anybody else what you write down as a loss. Don't be surprised if you have difficulty in identifying the losses involved. It may help you to break through that barrier if you try to think about all the regrets you have. You may find it easy to remember the large ones, but those that seem small may be even more important if you can 'look behind them' at what they represent for you. Name all the 'if onlys' and all the 'what ifs', no matter how small they may seem. They could point to something, or someone, much bigger. But take warning – this can be quite a shocking exercise.

Overcoming fear

Even when all is named and examined, the demoralizing effect of fear is still there – something that has to be overcome. We all face losses in life; if we cannot overcome fear how can we get beyond the shock stage as we experience them? There is a way to overcome fear. It involves playing a mind game with ourselves.

There is a question we have to answer: when we are faced by a threat of some kind but feel we lack the resources to overcome it, what do we do?

This is the game. Imagine some threats to yourself that would put you at risk of losing something or someone important to you – there are some examples below. Then plan how you would or could respond to that threat. In particular, think how you would bargain with another person. As you imagine different situations a pattern will emerge.

Here are some possible situations. Somebody pushes in front of you in a queue to buy some tickets that are in short supply for a popular show or concert. You suspect your partner is having an affair. A drunk threatens you or your partner with his fists out. The bank makes a mistake and deducts money from your account. A colleague at work or college makes a comment that puts you down unfairly. Now think of some more that you yourself have experienced, or others that you would not like to experience!

Write your spontaneous reactions down somewhere. (This is most important. You must get the imaginations out of your head and down onto paper. So if you have already run through these situations in your mind – go and get the sheet of paper and a pen now!) Once you have a scribbled outline of the sorts of reaction you tend to make when confronted with a threat, keep it hidden and then talk with others about how they would handle similar situations. Try to make a bit of a joke about it if you like. Observe television programmes and spot when the characters are suffering losses of one sort or another, then how they approach bargaining to restore those losses. Think about novels you have read and do the same. Now that you have gained some idea of how you naturally prefer to approach bargaining with other people to prevent or restore your losses, and how others might approach it in similar situations, you can look again at how you can overcome the demoralizing effect of fear.

The resource we need to overcome fear is not a weapon nor a defensive wall to hide behind. It is self-knowledge. In particular, it is the type of self-knowledge which can help each of us to gain a reasonable and achievable hope. In order to improve the way we can respond to threats with hope, and so overcome paralysing fear we need to know three things about ourselves. They are all linked to loss reactions. We need to know first, how we behave when we are *angry*; second, how we behave when we are *guilty*; and third, how we set about *bargaining*. Armed and protected by knowing this much about ourselves, we are in a good position to look another person in the eye, and hear what they have to say, and speak our own mind, and reflect on the effect of this without fear that the outcome will over-whelm us because hopefully we know enough about our own resources to handle even an unfavourable outcome. Afterwards we can learn some new ways for next time.

Understanding this 'game' throws light on a question that some people find difficult. What is the best way to use a period of engagement before marriage? It is not just for gathering furniture, and not for discovering whether we are sexually compatible. It is a time when two people get to know whether or not they can live with the way the other reacts when they are angry, and when they are guilty, and when they are bargaining. It is a time for honesty, and a time to learn if we are able to help each other heal through our losses.

At any stage in life, when the time comes to start looking at our relationship dependencies, it will be very helpful to have a wide vocabulary to name our feelings and our losses. Then we can identify and 'own' our subsequent grief, and recognize the grief of others as well, as we end that dependency and learn to become properly inter-dependent with each other instead. It may be worth glancing ahead now to the word lists in Chapter 9, particularly those which name the sorts of feelings in the Shock phase and in the Bargaining phase of loss reactions. Doing so could be helpful.

Overcoming the fears of feeling trapped, alone, in pain, and powerless

There are two things that make us most afraid. One is the possibility of being abandoned; the other is the danger of being oppressed. Fear of death is probably a mixture of both of these two most basic dreads. My experience in the surgery is that when confronted with the thought of their own impending death people's feelings of shock and fear are often about these, which then colour every aspect of life that comes to mind. At first they may resist experiencing these emotions in relationship to themselves; instead they rapidly shift their attention and project these feelings onto the effect their death will have on others. But later, when that focusing breaks down and the cry for life rises from every fibre of their own being, the fears of being abandoned and oppressed can assail them as four types of threat. These are the more specific fears which each one of us is going to need to develop resources to overcome. Here they are:

- feeling trapped,
- feeling alone,
- feeling pain,
- feeling powerless.

Just as we must prepare for the losses involved in marriage, so it is also a good idea to prepare for the losses involved in death. Marriage is, after all, the death of our independence, and not to be undertaken lightly as we generate a different sort of freedom in our life-long inter-dependence. To prepare for the losses involved in death we may also use the technique just described above. We need first to learn how we tend to react when we are *angry*, feel *guilty* and are *bargaining*. Then we can use that self-knowledge to learn how we can accept standing face to face with each of these feelings: being trapped . . . alone . . . in pain . . . and powerless.

So long as we cannot look these threats straight in the eye – and we all need to learn to do so – then to a certain extent we will be spending our lives running away from death and loss. This has important consequences. For to whatever extent we are denying facing up to our own death and losses, we will be dependent upon others, rather than inter-dependent with them in a healthy balance of acceptance. Things are very different once we have learnt to recognize our losses, and when we own our reactions to them. At that point, when we have accepted our limitations, we can each find a reasonable and achievable hope to live creative lives beyond fear.

CHAPTER 6

Physical Dependencies

Meeting our perceived needs either by physical means, or by relationship building

When we have a need – or feel that we have one – there are basically only two means to meet that need: either we build relationships, or we gather material of the world and use it. For example, after a row with a partner someone may choose either to get drunk or phone a trusted friend. I sometimes think of this choice between two means of meeting a need as a see-saw on which physical changes at one end are balanced with relationship changes at the other (Figure 2).

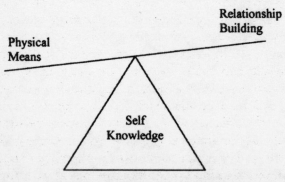

Figure 2   How we meet our needs

The choices we make depend largely upon how much we know about our own selves, which we may imagine to be hidden underneath the see-saw. Self-knowledge does affect our choices. As we think about ourselves and our needs, our minds will dwell on qualities of relationships or on physical things. Do I really want – or need – to get drunk, or could I choose to have time with my friend instead? Such thoughts – our 'bargaining style' – reveal themselves in the seemingly spontaneous decisions that we are continuously making.

Learning to have know-how, or wisdom

As we choose one or other of these routes (relationship or material satisfaction), so we increase our knowledge of the world around us. However, if we try to gain increasing understanding of and familiarity with the material world while trying to *deny* the impact of people upon its functioning, we will gain a very different type of understanding of life from that which arises if we are also able to concentrate upon the impact upon it of building relationships. Both routes will enable us to shape the physical world, but in different ways because of our different priorities and attitudes.

If we choose to apply ourselves, most of us could increase both our wisdom about people, and our knowledge, or 'know how' about the physical world. Experience, learning, training, listening, contemplation, prayer, and study, all come within that balancing triangle beneath the see-saw as ways to improve our understanding about ourselves, the world, and how people shape it. They all are means to improve the balance we can make between relationship building and handling our physical world. When we know more, we are better able to choose from a range of options, rather than choosing simply to allow our straightforward automatic reactions.

In this chapter we are considering how people sometimes focus their lives too much on their physical wants. Successfully balanced with wisdom about how people react to losses this may lead us to develop a reasonable pride in our know-how and ability to cope with the physical and material aspects of life. If associated with denial about relationship losses we risk a physical dependency. The alternative, when we are trying to recover from any physcial dependency, is to focus upon the way we go about relationship building. The wisdom involved in relationship building, surprisingly, is largely concerned with recognizing the diversity of the ways in which we all handle our losses.

The range of physical dependencies

To avoid all this thinking, however, there are many chemicals that simply alter the way our brains construct a picture of the world and our needs within it. These alterations might seem like progress or gain for a while, but with these sorts of apparent gains something else has to be lost. And so what seems like an easy way out comes hand in hand with unrecognized or even recognized loss reactions.

The types of chemical used to temporarily alter our quality of consciousness range from those that change our internal hormone balance (exercise highs, adrenaline stimulation, breath holding, fasting with sugar bingeing), through socially regulated chemicals (caffeine in tea and coffee, licensed alcohol and nicotine), and medically regulated prescribed drugs (analgesics, sedatives, antidepressants, anxiety drugs), to illegal street drugs and solvents. Most people explore some of these, often for fun, as part of that voyage of discovery of how they can enjoy the 'gathering' half of the life cycle. Many people quite reasonably make use of medication to pull themselves out of complications of complex losses into a gathering phase again.

Using chemicals as a physical means of meeting needs is thus initially concerned with what we may call 'thriving', but for some it may go on to become a matter of actual survival. At first the use of chemicals may be in balance with relationship building, but the attractive lack of effort involved in using them may mean that they become more appealing than the unpredictability of other people.

Exploring psychoactive chemicals in the form of illegal street drugs is dangerous – no less dangerous than it is to explore adrenaline effects stimulated by rock climbing. Climbing vast chunks of dust and consuming small amounts of dust are both physical means of meeting personal needs by getting 'a high'. Both can be done as shared events in which relationships are also being built. They can equally both be done in the peace of solitude. But the bravado that may be put on by somebody in a group may be a way of concealing personal losses. Deep down, underlying the bravado, there is often a sense of social isolation with a lingering sense of being alienated from the other people. If we recognize that feeling, it offers a clue that loss reactions are lurking and have built up to a complicated level. They need our attention. What usually happens, though, is that the bravado takes over instead. Social activity groups may practice a kind of 'one-upness'; on the other hand, illicit drug or alcohol groups may develop an inverted sort of 'one-down-ness'.

With both types of need-meeting physical activity there is a danger of coming down too fast! Rediscovering cold clammy reality can bring its own loss reaction, grief for the loss of that brief period of happy escape. Susceptible people, the ones who already have to cope with more than enough unresolved losses in their lives, are now at a greater risk of dependency. Such situations often give rise to physical dependencies – when the main hope of escape from the pain of pre-existing 'loss' reactions lies in 'gathering' some feature of the physical world. (This is not a strict medical definition, but a practical way of identifying how people get trapped by unresolved loss reactions.)

We have mentioned dependency upon externally taken chemicals; but this is only one type of physical dependency. Another is using physical means to alter our internal hormone balance, and the most accessible hormone for this is adrenaline. (Strictly speaking it is not adrenaline alone that gives the high which some people enjoy, but the accompanying release of stress associated steroid hormones as well.) The obvious means of driving the adrenaline system hard are strenuous exercise and danger seeking, but there are other more subtle ones, such as gambling, or, even more subtly, strategic money-making, e.g. financial dealing. These can become all-absorbing to the point of addictiveness at the expense of the relationship aspects of our human nature, and each can bring its own pattern of concealed loss reactions, as described in the last paragraph. These dependency pursuits bring with them an engulfing trap of eternal unfulfilment.

One final pattern of physical dependency needs mentioning. Sexuality is amongst the highest forms of human sensitivity when it involves person to person exploration. When there is a degree of alienation, however, and physical dependency takes over, then sensitivity corrupts into sensuality. Other *people* may become mere sex *objects* instead, and obsessional behaviour is not far away. People who complain about the purveying of sexuality as a commodity are often dismissed as 'moralizers'. But it is quite reasonable to point out that this way of coping with loss fails to lead people on from their immediate sense of need towards a greater joy in our shared full humanity. Sadly the 'moralizers' sometimes make this point in an insensitive or unreasonable way, or are perceived as being judgmental or downright killjoys. Far from 'killing joy', accepting their advice is likely to improve human well-being by enhancing and sustaining person-to-person sensitivity.

Failing to be honest with another person as the root of physical dependencies

We have mentioned two methods of meeting needs: relationship building and physical changes. Either can be pushed to an extreme. For some people the see-saw will have swung so far out of balance that the losses involved become noticeable to others if not to themselves. For example, if somebody joins a cult their relationship dependency is likely to become all-absorbing. When working with people who have left cults I have found it is important to provide as many means of experimenting with physical activities as possible, so that the see-saw can gradually swing back and find a new balance. Likewise, when somebody has developed a dependency on drugs or other psychoactive chemicals, usually underlying it there is a problem with relationship building. When counselling such a person it is important not only to offer help with breaking habits, but also to concentrate upon how to improve choices about honesty in relationship building. This is of the utmost importance in bringing about recovery. Until that choice is active, no recovery can be expected.

Physical dependency as a form of denial of loss

Multiple loss reaction analysis can be very helpful, or very challenging, for somebody who is trying to overcome a physical dependency. The challenge arises because the physical dependency habit is a learned method of denying losses. A further complication is that these losses are often being denied as a way of avoiding the need to be honest, or open, with some other person.

When people deny their losses the emotions involved re-surface in a variety of different patterns in different people. Most people who are physically dependent suspect they are somehow harming themselves, particularly those with chemical dependencies, and do not mind doing that. In such cases, guilt tinged with anger can be emerging as this drive towards self-harm. Escaping from the guilt-anger whirlpool within the loss reaction may lead people back into denial behaviour. They may instead need to forgive themselves for some act of weakness, but deciding to follow that route is too complicated and painful – after all, the chemical is there at hand to numb the confusing feelings of reality. In a competitive world admitting to weakness and limits could be dangerous, so that the honesty needed to accept our limits, which make us different from others, comes to seem a luxury. 'Even if I were to accept my loss of self-respect, why should others forgive me rather than reject me? The risks are terrifying. And how can I face all this if I also have to lose the comfort of my habit and the pleasure I get?'

This book does not provide a programme to overcome chemical dependencies or other types of physical dependency. But the framework within which successful programmes are already operating does include an honest self-appraisal. It is possible to gain this kind of self-knowledge by means of the structured multiple loss analysis outlined in this book. Certainly an understanding of one's own personal pattern of loss reaction, gained over an extended period of time, would be a very valuable possession. In order to help in gaining this kind of self-understanding we now turn to two important features of life: the nature of forgiveness, and the reason why forgiveness is so healing.

The nature of forgiveness

We all hurt others sometimes, and can feel especially bad about hurting those we love even though they may have hurt us first. Owning our part in straining that relationship can be very difficult when we would perhaps find it safer to blame the other – although admittedly sometimes it is very unclear whether or not we did do anything to cause a problem. When struggling with such feelings we may look at our fingernails or repeatedly cross one set of toes over the other – anything physical to ease the emotional strain within. We do something similar also on a much bigger scale – anything physical will do to divert attention while I am having difficulty being honest about my role in this mess. 'Let's get lost in this activity.' In fact, getting used to this technique means 'the bolder I am as I do it, the better it diverts attention!'

When physical *dependency* sets in, this method of delaying honesty has been developed to a fine art. To step out from behind the physical screen, to make an honest assessment of our limits in relationships, would leave us 'in the raw' and plagued by guilty feelings that have grown out of all proportion to the importance of any original relationship problems. By delaying, there is thus a 'priming' of the guilt stage of loss reactions for those who have become dependent upon having a physical screen to hide behind, and this can provide a background complication to our processing of all subsequent losses. To avoid a recurrence of 'that questioning feeling' during our reactions to any subsequent risks of loss, which reminds us of some former inter-personal difficulty, physical dependents may find it far more preferable to remain in the anger and denial phases. This guilty-angry-denial whirlpool can then create a drive to words self harming and, in denial, to words projecting that anger or harm onto others.

So here is the trap: to move on from denial and anger, we need to *pass through* guilty feelings. Now if we are honest with ourselves, we know that there is no drug, good deed or sensual comfort which permanently dissolves away guilty feelings. We know, but have difficulty acknowledging, that the only enduring cure for feeling guilty is forgiveness. Shifting guilt onto somebody else is not a cure. But why on earth *should* I forgive somebody else when they may have been at fault, or even why *should* I forgive myself?

In Chapter 2 I described how loss reactions do not proceed simply through the list from one stage to another. All sorts of whirlpools are possible, and even leaps from one stage to another. Forgiveness is, in fact, one of these leaps. Forgiveness is the leap from anger directly into mature acceptance. That is why we *should* forgive, because it completes our loss reactions and fills out our more mature character. But it isn't as easy as that.

Forgiving is often so difficult, because packed inside it is fear, doubt, anger, guilt, yearning, bargaining, and the powerless despair of depression. If we cannot truly forgive in one leap, then we must work slowly through to true acceptance of our situation where we know freedom again, or remain trapped ourselves. When we forgive somebody, we give life to them by saying that despite my loss I am powerless to change you *other than by releasing you*. This method of complex loss reaction analysis is, when all is said and done, a way of spreading out forgiveness over time. 'Children,' remarked Oscar Wilde, 'begin by loving their parents; after a time they judge them; rarely, if ever, do they forgive them.' If any of us remain snagged at the anger stage, then physical dependency is one way of diverting attention from this truth: we need to find some way of forgiving for things to change from the roots upwards.

People can usually handle their anger more easily if they have some idea of where it can resolve. It ultimately resolves into the forgiveness of mature acceptance. It could almost be pictured like sap rising from the roots of a tree and creating the spreading crown that casts shade for others to rest from the heat of the sun and branches for children to play in. Although that may create a rather static image of life, in our activity the anger of loss can provide the energy we need to push through the depressive elements of bargaining into true acceptance of our limited but beneficial spread in life. It is a more creative use of anger than self harm, but if I am to direct my energy this way there is a basic truth I must realize: we need to sense how our thriving does inter-depend on the thriving of others.

Forgiveness is important for our thriving. We need to be clear about the meaning of the word. Forgiveness is often confused with pardon. *Pardon* means freeing somebody from the legal consequences of their wrong action without penalties. It is possible, of course, to *forgive* somebody (including oneself) without expecting to be let off punishment for wrongdoing. The difference is the same as that between mercy and leniency, which we looked at before. The fellow-feeling we call mercy, like forgiveness, is an act of neighbourly love. On the other hand leniency, like pardon, require reasoning to work out if a possible course of action really is in the best interests of those concerned in any given situation. Why should I make these points? It is to clarify that leniency and pardon are options to make the 'gathering' phase of the life cycle creative, whereas mercy and forgiveness are essentials if we are to make the 'loss' half of the cycle creative. Loss only becomes creative if we begin to sense the fellow-feeling which turns mercy and forgiveness into inter-dependent thriving with others.

For me to forgive somebody or myself involves 'loss' because it means accepting that I am powerless to control this other person or my own unruly heart. Then, having accepted that and before that person shows any sign of making amends to me, I give him or her freedom. Forgiveness is, in effect, '[be]fore giving' of freedom, before amends have been made to me. Offering it requires a deep confidence. I need to trust that the ways of the world and the ways of people are such that *in time* they will realize the harm they cause and choose of their own free will to change. Despite all short term difficulties, this remains a reasonable and merciful hope.

Granting pardon involves the choice whether or not to withhold punishment, and as such is an action. In contrast to this, the essential element of a wider trust in forgiveness means that we could think of forgiveness as a type of prayer.

Giving importance to the loss of pleasure

In addition to realizing the importance of forgiveness, we need to focus on a second feature when using multiple loss analysis for physical dependency. Whether shaking free of *dependency* upon chemicals or adrenaline or sensuality, there will be a very significant loss of pleasure. Is there any way in which this can be made up or compensated for? There is one way to achieve this: the loss of pleasure can only be made up for by a growing experience of pleasure within the realm of relationship building. In this context it is dishonesty which robs us of pleasure that would otherwise be ours. Any act of dishonesty so disrupts this building of relationships that the building site of someone's life can become a rocky shambles. A close look at how we go about relationship building becomes extremely important if we want to ensure that honesty leads to pleasure and not only to punishment.

This is such an important issue that it is the subject of the whole third part of this workbook.

CHAPTER 7

Hopelessness

In the previous chapters we have looked at some of the types of reaction people have to loss and to the risk of loss. It may be helpful to summarize them here.

- First we looked at the emotional overload and burn-out that comes with multiple losses.
- Then we looked at trying to restore our losses by repeatedly controlling some aspect of our own behaviour instead of bargaining to change the world 'out there' which has come to seem so immovable.
- Next we looked at two basic types of dependency among which we might try to hide:
  1. Dependency in our relatedness when we choose not to see how we are allowing others to live our lives for us; and
  2. Dependency in our physical environment when we choose to boost our short term present experience in order not to have to think too much about our losses.

There is one final reaction we need to look at before considering how we can find a steadier balance between the losing and gathering parts of the life cycle. It is the reaction that follows when, along with everything else, we also lose hope.

Three models of depression

'Depression' is a term that is used very loosely. The popular idea of a mood state of feeling black, hopeless and uncommunicative is only one aspect, and perhaps not the most important one. The technical name for these temporary swings of mood is *dysphoria* (pronounced dis-FORia) rather than depression. Depressions are more prolonged, are self-perpetuating, and are associated with more disturbance of bodily functions such as sleep pattern, appetite, sexual drive, bowel function and so on. In fact, from a medical point of view clinical depression is often thought of as a depressed biochemistry in which subtle changes of hormone levels can be detected by research workers (not in tests done by GPs). That is why a clinical depression cannot respond to will power or to a 'pull yourself together' response, which may well be effective for a dysphoria.

True clinical depression is a potentially fatal condition. People in depression may kill themselves, and so it becomes quite important to distinguish dysphoria from depression. In fact, in modern western culture the main causes of young death are no longer diseases and malnutrition. Science and technology have cured that successfully, but the cost has been a culture that has lost something in its heart, so that now the main causes of young death are suicide and accidents. To cure that epidemic we need to help people find their own hearts and relate heart-to-heart. One simple but effective way to distinguish when somebody is having a mood swing and when they are medically depressed is this: it is very rare for people in a dysphoria to have ideas about killing themselves. If anybody has started to think seriously about suicide, rather than just a fleeting thought about the prospect, then there is a clinical depression that has deepened to the point of needing some sort of medical treatment.

Self-perpetuating depression that would benefit from medical treatment does exist without suicidal thoughts but, for relatives and friends of the sufferer, this is the most important point to distinguish. How do you find out? Simply by asking. Do so confidently as a true, friendly enquiry, heart-to-heart. You will not, repeat not, push somebody into an attempted suicide merely by asking. They will have thought about it long before you, and it is far more likely that you will receive an expression of profound relief that somebody has cared enough to notice and ask. If it is a mood swing the notion of suicide will be quickly disowned by the sufferer. If there is a clinical depression the sufferer may feel frightened that such thoughts should be occurring, and will probably be grateful for the suggestion (please note) that you go along to the doctor with them and wait in the waiting room while they go in.

I remember a situation where a woman came to see me because of her husband's depressive mood. He was refusing to talk with anybody about what was wrong. Most men have the same difficulty overcoming that resistance to admitting they cannot control it on their own. When I suggested she offer to come with him to a joint appointment she was surprised at the idea, but delighted to discover he readily agreed. For him this was the sign of co-operation he had been looking for, rather than pressure to do something that only further emphasized how unhappy he was with himself. We were able to talk completely openly about his suicidal ideas, and from that point they simply left him. He no longer felt unsafe with himself, and discovered for himself how talking with a stranger could improve his sense of self-value. It was a long haul from there, but a good start.

For the purposes of this self-help book I am going to describe three different types of depression. The survey will not be exhaustive. I am not, for instance, going to include post-natal depression, nor manic depression, nor the existential depression that may come with questioning the whole meaning and value of one's present existence. These all have special features of their own which may be independent of, or co-exist with, the ones described here. The three to be described, however, are all associated with the way in which a person has become stuck as they cope with their loss reactions, and they may be helped by multiple loss reaction analysis.

1. Repressed anger

This type of depression has already been mentioned. Children sometimes grow up in homes where they learn that expression of feelings (especially anger) is taboo in their family, or brings an even more frightening response from somebody. As a result, in later life, they repress strong feelings because they seem unsafe. Repression might be a reasonable survival technique for children, but if the technique is used inappropriately in adult life, then problems may result. As adults particularly we all need a little assertive drive to negotiate a proper balance in life, both with other adults and to bring up children to be socially responsible people. It is worth noting in this context that a form of repressive depression can be found among some churchgoers who remain depressed because they have been mistakenly taught in the church that all anger is wrong. They may have been incited on noting some injustice, but have learned to suppress their anger. In trying to bury it, they become despondent and depressed. This attitude to anger can breed a sort of lame Christianity that puts many men off church life. Yet a hundred years ago the opposite was true; the church was the safe and effective place to express and act on our hostile reactions to social injustice.

Some of us may need to unlearn the idea that assertiveness is going to lead to harm. But if we are to be assertive we must believe in our own self-worth as well as the worth of others. This is where depression becomes a trap, fixing an idea of our loss of worthiness to assert that drive to change the world around us. If we pick up the idea that others are more worthy than us, rather than as worthy as us, we are heading for trouble. (We are also heading for trouble if we come to believe that they are less worthy than us!) There is all the difference in the world between recognizing that somebody else has greater need than us, and believing that somebody else is of greater worth than us.

Very often the anger that is repressed is a righteous anger at injustice when we recognize that somebody's need is being ignored by others. It makes a difference, for example, how we respond if we see somebody being victimized at work and can recognize a time in our past when we ourselves were victimized. Do we now turn our anger assertively into some creative comment, or do we silently let our memory burn again within us? Humanity is poorer if it is not expressed and acted upon. In fact if we express that anger it may be the gift of life to others, even though we will risk loss of security for ourselves in the process. Not to act upon it may even harden our hearts as we 'bottle it up'. What can we do to change if we recognize we have a problem in this area? We start by doing a complex loss reaction analysis to work out how we handle our grief, then learn to name our feelings, and then plan out how we can handle the loss of security by building relationships heart-to-heart.

When repressed anger is self-destructively causing a dysphoria or depression, and the depression starts to lift, the denied anger will then inevitably be expressed in some way. Often it will be expressed at people who are trusted, who represent a safe place to experiment with fire. It can be very helpful if the relatives and friends of the sufferer understand this so that they do not misinterpret it and become self-justifying in response. What is expressed is anger at loss, not anger at you. To simply accept the anger's expression, especially in recovery from depression, and to demonstrate to the person that they are still acceptable to you after it, may even help to prevent a recurrence of a depressive pattern at some later time as the sense of mutual worth grows stronger. The technique for relatives and friends is simple. Just as in a football game the principle is, 'Don't go for the player, go for the ball', so likewise in depression the principle is, 'Don't go for the feeling, go for the loss.' Rather than argue about the anger or the moodiness, recognize these as features of loss reactions and work out which loss is bothering them. Then you can negotiate how to restore the important feature of that loss, and help them to ditch the unimportant aspects of it that really should be left behind.

Tragically, recovery from a deep depression of this type can also be fraught with danger. When the brain chemistry is beginning to work more efficiently, whether or not anti-depressant tablets have been used to unlock the bio-chemical trap, the sense of powerlessness begins to lift. If this happens before the person's sense of worth has begun to improve, then disaster may follow. The sufferer feels motivated to take action with the anger, but takes action against their self. The drive to suicide may arise just as people think the person is beginning to get better and is taking more interest in life. It is important to see that the seeds of this action lie not in the way you or anybody else is relating to the depressed person, but right back in the way that person has been unable to learn how to apply their anger gently and constantly in balance with others of equal worth.

2. The whirlpool of shame – repressing guilt

The depression phase of loss was described in the first part of this book as growing sense of our powerlessness as gambits we employ to restore our losses, fail and our yearning turns to hopelessness. This is a true dysphoria and is not in itself a medical problem. But for some people who have a depressive tendency this phase may trip a grief reaction into a recurrence of self-perpetuating clinical depression. It may occur when the depressive phase of grief gets tied up with guilt in another of these unhelpful whirlpools of emotion – a cycle of depression-guilt that we know as shame.

It is worth looking at three features of personality that can contribute to tripping shame into a clinical depression. The first is this: when a non-depressed person experiences loss they are likely to identify the cause of that loss as 'out there'. If for example somebody has had a bad day at work, then the non-depressive is likely to say it was because the boss was in a bad mood and was taking it out on other people. A person with a depressive tendency, on the other hand, is more likely to locate the cause of the bad day as 'in here', and to think the boss was being difficult because there was something wrong with their own work performance. Somebody suffering from depression often has a tendency to 'internalize' the cause of problems.

Secondly, the non-depressive is more able to see each problem as a specific event with unique features. The non-depressive would say that the boss is in a bad mood because his wife is ill and he is having problems getting the children off to school, whereas the depressive is more likely to say that the boss is getting at him because his work is usually not up to standard, and not just his work but his life generally is in a mess. There is a tendency to 'generalize' the cause of problems in depressive thought patterns.

Thirdly, the non-depressive is more able than the depressive to be able to put a time limit on the cause of the depression. The non-depressive would say that the situation will improve when the boss's wife is out of hospital, while the depressive would say that even when the boss's wife is out of hospital it won't be any different because my work performance in life generally has always been bad, and always will be bad. In a depressive thought pattern the causes of loss tend to become 'fixed'.

This tendency to see the causes of problems as internalized, generalized, and fixed is often associated with recurrent depressive thought patterns. If you reflect for a moment on those features you will see that they each have the effect of laying the blame for a set of events inside oneself rather than out in the world. In fact they show all the features of *the guilt stage of loss reactions* we have previously looked at. Therefore we could say that long-term unresolved guilty feelings can contribute to a tendency to recurrent depressions, and that loss reaction analysis might therefore help a person to move on from that stage.

Now this is the exact parallel of the repressed and unresolved anger we looked at previously. Here we have two different types of depression, both of which can arise from unresolved and probably unrecognized loss reactions. One represents an anger-denial cycle of repression. The other is a depression-guilt cycle of shame. Earlier in the book we encountered the guilt-anger whirlpool which can spin off its energy as obsessional behaviour, and here we encounter two other important whirlpools that can consume all our mental energy into a depression as we cease to struggle through our grief.

This insight into how our emotions may become self-perpetuating opens up a new possibility to re-assess the picture we have of ourselves in the world. We can take a loss reaction analysis approach to ourselves by naming the losses which we still feel bad about, recognizing the feelings we have about each one of them, and talking about our resources to move them on openly. When I took this approach with a man who was suffering a dreadfully deep depression in retirement, we discovered in the midst of his list an item where, in the midst of an outrage about how events were stacking up against him when he was running a business, he had angrily done something illegal. In doing this he had lost his self-respect as a previously honest man. Naming the losses of self-respect, identity and power, and focusing on those rather than on his feelings about the legality or illegality of his actions, was one of the most important steps in a prolonged process that led to recovery. He had fixed the idea in his head that to have done such a thing he must always have been an evil and weak-willed man and that everything he did was therefore tainted by his ability to behave in this way. Of course it was not true, but only by looking at his own personal style of loss reaction could we start getting him to see that.

Two questions lie heavy at the heart of someone who is experiencing loss reactions stuck in the phase of guilt. One is, 'What did I do to cause that loss?' The other is, 'What could I have done to have prevented that loss?' The answers to both questions is usually, 'Nothing!' The sense of loss is tragedy, an inescapable part of the life cycle to which we with other equally human beings must adjust. Once we have come to recognize our own humanity as something we share with other people who are struggling – like us – to prevent the sense of loss, we can allow ourselves to attribute more worth to all involved. We are also more likely to take the risks needed to bargain through our loss reactions in order either to restore the important losses or to accept that our life can be creative even as we minimize the losses for each other, and so recover true depth of personal relationships.

By now the importance of effective bargaining about losses may be becoming clearer, although not yet, perhaps, how to go about it. Effective bargaining is the stage which is missing from all three whirlpools. We shall look more closely at bargaining towards the end of this chapter, and it is the theme running through the whole final section of the book. But first we need to be aware of the third type of depression that can be associated with unrecognized and unresolved loss reactions.

3. Learned helplessness

Some families experience more depression through the different generations than others. It is very difficult for researchers to work out whether this pattern is inherited or something that is learned in the family. Almost certainly both influences are at work simultaneously, so even when a genetic link is clear it should be seen as only one factor among others that might pre-dispose someone to depression. There is nothing inevitable about it.

What sorts of things can be socially learned that would predispose someone to depression? Apart from the problems of learning unhelpful ways of handling anger and guilt (with the associated under-development of bargaining or negotiating skills as a result) there is another socially learned problem which should be looked out for. The message some people pick up from others is that 'you really needn't bother to fight for whatever it is you value because you don't stand a chance of winning it – better give up now and save yourself the trouble later'. Such messages are about one thing – powerlessness. They may come from competitors, but they may also come from friends, and even more difficult, they may come from family. The message also implies: 'If you try to gain this, then you will lose our support, and probably also our respect.' This message puts the hearer in a sort of a double bind. Whichever direction they move, they are going to experience loss. That, at any rate, is how the situation may seem to those susceptible to this type of manipulation.

This type of manipulative social context often leads the 'victim' to confuse freedom with independence. The hope of gaining freedom might inspire someone to break out of these harmful relationships; but they may run the risk of discovering that mere generalized independence from other people doesn't provide the whole answer to their problem. On the other hand, until they have made that bid for freedom, people in double binds can be susceptible to depressions because they get into the habit of anticipating their own powerlessness.

For example, I can think of a young woman who was always being criticized for not coming up to expectations in her family. She was getting depressed, and decided to leave home and move into her own flat in the nearby city. The parents said it would never work, but she made the bargaining gambit to go and restore her lost self-respect. She started to meet young men, and took up with one who seemed to be strong when she felt herself to be weak. He eventually moved in with her, and then progressively started to dominate her life, until she found she was repeating the pattern of being criticized that she had experienced at home. Eventually it all went sadly wrong, and she asked to move back to the parents' house. They took her back, of course, but made her realize that they had seen it coming!

Just reading about it is depressing – and she did become depressed again! It is a tricky situation to get out of, and many people feel they need to put about two hundred miles between themselves and that power drain in order to feel themselves normal again. Others find they are able to handle it even though they may remain in the same geographical area, provided that they find an alternative set of relationships in which they can develop their bargaining and negotiating skills with self-respect. Having achieved this they can apply these skills to the power-draining manipulative relationships. Sadly this drive to get an alternative set of relationships sometimes swings to the opposite extreme, such as gang mentality or cult membership.

Alternatively many people go through two or three moderately long and deeply harmful relationships before they recognize they have a pattern of selecting bad partners. The answer to this is to name the losses that have shaped your tendency to set your hopes on another person, and work through the loss reactions before you fall for another partner.

But what exactly is lost when the messages of powerlessness are being given? Learned helplessness induces the despair of depression when we lose hope. Because relationship building requires hope, to truly lose hope is a crushing experience. Losing hope is the loop which can spring the snare of clinical depression. Losing hope drains our energy to try out changes which might just discover new areas where joy can grow within the free struggle of making relationships work. We cannot conjure up hope. Illusions are not built from true relationships. A depressed person is snared because he or she knows better than anybody that illusory hopes are worthless, ignited as they are from relationships that have not touched the depths. It may seem odd to want to talk to a depressed person about loss and how to handle it, but to everybody's surprise it cuts through illusions like a warm knife through butter. It is the path to deep relationships, built over time with honesty.

Medication may be needed to break the snare of clinical depression. Anti-depressant tablets do not work by creating an artificial mood. They slowly boost the normal chemistry of the brain and over time give the person more mental energy to see their way through relational problems and to analyse situations more clearly. How each individual applies that mental energy remains up to them, within their choice as their energy and imagination for choices increases. Mood improves as people see through the preoccupations, illusions, and delusional ideas that they hold onto with the force of conviction until they can honestly see that there is another hope. Deliverance comes if, as we emerge from the power-lessness of depression, we find others are there with whom to make this honest hope into reality. Then the chances are much increased that that joy of being deeply known and accepted will thrive in a more prolonged or sustained manner. At the very least, the ability to adjust better to a temporary loss of joy will be our permanent possession.

The difference between losing hope and living without hope

I spent some time going through a loss reaction analysis with one person to try to penetrate a curious sense of joy-lessness that she was experiencing. To an outsider her life would have seemed full of present experience, and yet to her it lacked any substantial value. She was not clinically depressed, and she had several active friendships. All the losses we could identify had been worked through to acceptance, which fitted with her ready ability to make friendships. It seemed a strange contrast to discover that when she was young she had had a very difficult and bro-ken family life with many disappointments. She seemed well adjusted to those losses, and seemed to have genuinely forgiven those involved. What could explain her joyless-ness? I thought, 'If you encounter an emotion that is part of the loss reaction sequence, then there is some unresolved loss in the background. Don't dwell on the feeling. Identify and name the loss *as a loss*, not as a wish-for or a fear-of but as a named loss (that is the difficult bit), and then push on across the stepping stones for that loss.'

With some gentle encouragement we discovered some-thing that gave her a shock. As a child she had grown so afraid of losing hope that she had developed a survival tech-nique – which she was still unwittingly using. To survive she had decided to live without hope. Hope spans time, and we need time to find the reality of each other. If we decide to live without hope we cannot find the reality of each other, and so life will come to seem valueless.

I do not believe this person had truly lost hope as such, rather she had made a conscious and purposeful choice to live without it. Her shock reaction hinted that recalling this memory, and realizing the importance of surviving by it, had brought with it a risk of insecurity. She suddenly faced the risk of losing her security. Her survival technique had worked for the time span of many years, but now in order to thrive fully as a free person she was going to have to lose her defence.

Suicidal drives as protest

Loss of hope, not loss of defence, is central to the tragedy of depression. When this happens, fleeting suicidal ideas may become obsessionally fixed. Attempted or successful suicide is the most extreme form of passing one's own grief onto others. The questions will echo for a lifetime in the hearts of those who have lost a relative or friend through suicide. Why did they not say before? Could I have done something to prevent it? It really is true that we can only ever make guesses about what is going on in another person, and those who are closest to us do still hide from us. It takes openness on both sides, defenceless listening, to bridge that gap. But even then, no matter how much we know and are knowing about another, we must always have to interpret what we feel and see. Our interpretations may get better with time, or we may come up against a limit. Do we then feel empty and stop trying, feel disillusioned perhaps?

In there may be the clue to understanding a drive to commit suicide. We, in our daily routines, can stop trying to interpret or change others because of our temporary disillusionment. What of others? There are many who guess that the drive to suicide is a result of a similar giving up. But I doubt that that is, in fact, the best guess we can make. The drive to suicide is too active for that. Another guess is this, that the drive to suicide is a protest, an angry and self-critical shout in outrage that life should be like this. It could be likened more to opting for strike action in an industrial dispute.

Protest as a sign of hope, but a failure of bargaining

Seeing the drive to suicide as a protest, not as giving up, opens up the possibility of identifying if there is a weak spot in handling loss reactions that has predisposed the person to such an action. It would thus place this drive within a wider context of normal living, rather than outside the context of normal living as something fearfully uncontrollable. It makes sense of the fact that anybody can get fleeting ideas of suicide without it meaning the onset of madness, and it can show how to move on from them.

To make a protest there must be some remaining spark of hope. To make a protest there must be some outrage, however slight. To turn that outrage against one's self, there must be some questioning of one's own role and capabilities. To make a protest in such a way is to say that hope, anger and doubt are co-existing, and also to say that I do not see how else to bargain or negotiate my way out of this situation.

The suicidal drive is really a failure of the bargaining stage of loss adjustment. It is a blind dash through the complexity of bargaining with all of its further risk of losses. Hope has been misplaced from finding true openness of relationships into proving one's own powerfulness, even if it is the last thing I do. Attempted suicide is often thought of as a cry for help, and sometimes it may be just that. But for what sort of help is the appeal being made? If it is a manipulative gesture to force someone to continue cosseting when they had begun to slip, then to respond to the manipulation by giving in to the demand can hardly be called help. If it is an appeal for somebody to do something for me, then it is doubtful that that sort of help would have any lasting effect other than to trap the sufferer in the same mental frame.

The cry for help in a suicidal gesture is not just a cry for support. It is a cry of protest that my powers of bargaining are not sufficient. Enough of illusions! Let us all find reality by shattering the illusion of right relationships! The cry is for help in broadening my ability to bargain and negotiate our loss of honesty. It is a desperate gambit to make others lose their illusions of me, if necessary by losing me, because I lack the skills to make it any other way.

Aggressive, assertive and passive bargaining

The two stepping stones in the loss reaction towards which it is best to aim are bargaining or acceptance. It does not matter much which, as long as you are clear for which you are aiming, and have identified which of your losses you are dealing with. Not everybody can aim straight for acceptance. The forgiveness involved may be too complex and painful, and then it needs stretching out as a grieving process. Bargaining is an inevitable feature of living together in society, and we are all poorer people in a culture that has lost the desire and ability to give and take. Why bargain and risk loss when you can stake an outright claim for 'rights' to which somebody will listen?

This brings us back to bargaining styles, and the skills we could develop to broaden our methods. People may take an *aggressive* approach to bargaining, or a *passive* approach, or try to find the middle way of an *assertive* approach to bargaining. The ideal is probably the wide middle ground of assertiveness. This is an attitude in which both oneself and the other person are equally valued as worthy people. In assertiveness there needs to be an open statement of one's needs and hopes even though these may not be to the other's liking, and these statements are balanced with an ability to listen to those of the other person without feeling a shock-laden doubt about one's resources to cope. It involves time to reflect, without feeling that pressure of time to be threatening. That sense of pressure may be the fact of building a relationship over time. In this assertive state reasonable compromises can be found which minimize loss, and maximize gain for all involved. Assertive bargaining involves the risk of gradually lowering one's defences. When people are unwilling to take that risk, bargaining methods veer defensively towards either the aggressive extreme or the passive extreme.

The bargaining word list in Chapter 9 is divided into three columns which correspond with the aggressive, assertive, and passive styles of bargaining. By ticking those which you can imagine yourself using you will gain a picture of which style you tend to use. The ideal way to develop your bargaining skills is not by trying to avoid using passive or aggressive methods – it is by actively experimenting with assertive methods. It is true that there may be situations where extreme aggression or extreme passivity are useful techniques to prevent or restore loss. If they can be used selectively then there is no problem. If, however, we lack any other method of bargaining, then in the long run we shall find that they are likely to generate more problems than they solve.

Loss of hope is only one part of the story of depression, but an important one. Loss of the ability to bargain in a situation fraught with illusions is an even more important one. What hope, then, is there for us in the glittering success of a technologically advanced western culture when it is accompanied by a massive increase in suicide among young- and middle-aged people? Where is the illusion in all that? Perhaps the third part of this book will provide some pointers for ways to redress the balance, as we look more closely at the role of bargaining and negotiating in the building of true relationships.

PART 3

FINDING THE REALITY OF EACH OTHER

CHAPTER 8

Relationship Building

In his ground-breaking book *The Sixty Minute Father*, Rob Parsons quotes a wise saying – 'It has never yet been recorded that anybody has spoken the dying words, "I wish I had spent more time at the office." '

That anecdote sums up the theme of this final part of the book. I am simply going to tease out a few ideas about how we could spend some of that 'saved time' going for the real gold of life – the relationship building of friendship. Even husbands and wives need to learn to be friends!

Building with hope, present experience and loss

Many people think of relationships as comforting and nurturing – relationships make us feel good. But having a good relationship and building a good relationship are two entirely different things. It may take some people many years to realize that good relationships need to be built over time, and because of this they need to change their attitude to relationships. What I say to my patients is that building a relationship starts at 20 per cent hope, 20 per cent present experience, and 60 per cent loss.

Why is there so much loss? The reason is that for every decision I make to do something to build a relationship, I am simultaneously choosing not to do at least one other thing that I would otherwise have chosen to do for myself. Such choices remain hidden – to ourselves sometimes, and to others. As Robert Burns wrote:

> 'What's done we partly may compute,
> But know not what's resisted.'

At some level, that choice not to do something for myself must bring a loss reaction in its wake. I may be able to adjust quickly, but if instead I deny these losses, then the reactions remain hibernating and re-emerge on occasions to wreak havoc. This explains why in an argument sometimes things from many years ago are sometimes brought up that have nothing to do with the present issue, and the whole exchange gets blown out of all proportion. The increased emotion is due to *unresolved loss reactions* resurfacing.

Because building any relationship must involve several losses, the loss reactions connected with a relationship are likely to be complex ones. While building relationships each of us will be getting to know our own unique way of reacting to our losses and bargaining about them, and also guessing how the person we are relating to is uniquely reacting. The whole process can thus be doubly complicated. In fact, given that we and others are always throughout our lives maturing and changing, there is enough to keep us going for a whole lifetime if we really work at building and re-negotiating our constant relationships.

If we fail to recognize that arguments are attempts to bargain through complex loss reactions, then an impression can mistakenly develop that two people are incompatible with each other. Repeated failure at bargaining leads to a low self-image, which in outrage can be blamed upon the other. Relationship breakdown, separation, divorce, drifting, fear of commitment, and loneliness can all follow from not recognizing that if the losses involved in a relationship are denied by one or the other party then the relationship is being built on an unstable foundation. Often what is actually sought in an argument is not so much victory over the other person, but simply to win the recognition that sustaining the relationship has involved loss or giving up. To show that we know that, and to show respect for the other's willingness to experience loss for our sake, is often all that is needed.

The one who gives up something will lose a certain amount of self-respect, and unless there is compensation in terms of improved present experience of the relationship, this loss of self-respect may lead to an irritable need to win another argument. When that experience of respect is absent from a marriage, or any significant relationship, hatred creeps in. But on the other hand where such respect is present then there grows a giving of life to each other. This giving-and-receiving is the basis of 'one-fleshness' in marriage – to use the phrase found in the marriage service and in Genesis (2:24) – and likewise of unity of heart in friendship.

Western culture has developed a pattern of prime relationships known as 'serial monogamy'. In such a relationship each of the two people expects that the other will remain loyal, but only until one feels that their needs are no longer being met by the other person. Then they find somebody else who meets their present set of needs with whom they can form another liaison, thus ending the previous relationship. In serial monogamy I respect the other person because their strengths can meet my weaknesses. Only 'the gatherer' is respected. Where there is no dignity of respect for each others' losses, there can be no well-founded relationship. This is not so much a 'one-flesh' relationship but a dependency. People think they are being mature by living together, but often they cling to what is in fact a child-like hope – namely, that their relationships should be comforting, nurturing experiences. Seen in this way, relationships are supposed to make us feel good, and if we do not feel good then it means there must be something wrong with the relationship. To abandon the other person is a denial reaction; in doing so we are trying to avoid the unpleasant truth that in order to find something lasting beyond ourselves we need to experience loss.

Being able to talk and listen in a non-judgemental way about losses, both those of others and our own, is an important way of keeping the present experience of relationship building above the 20 per cent mentioned above. It is important to realize that this 'twenty per cent present experience' of relationship building does not have to be comfortable or entertaining to be real. If we avoid it and self-indulgently dwell on the losses and on our unfulfilled hopes, then the 'sixty per cent loss reaction' element increases instead, and consumes our hope and present experience as we withhold from the other. Separation of heart becomes inevitable, and physical separation will probably follow.

The alternative route is to take the risk of discovering how, as we build a relationship, the quality of our 'twenty per cent present experience' can include talking about loss with love, and this can balance those times when we talk about gathering with reason. Resetting our hopes for the relationship to include a larger element of helping the other through previously unrecognized losses means we must also think about our own losses without shame. As we get to know our own pattern of bargaining to limit our losses, and how others bargain to limit theirs, the loss reaction analysis gives us a common language we can use with our partner to work through the difficult maze of emotions as we lose whatever may be preventing us from growing together. If we can learn to name our feelings openly when we are in anger or guilt or depression, this can alert our partner to the fact that what we are doing is building the relationship, not just complaining. Similarly if we recognize or suspect that our partner is experiencing these feelings in connection with some incident, then we can open up a depth of mutual respect by naming these feelings – but only when the words we employ carry no sense of criticism or judgment about wrongdoing. It is then that we begin to discover how true freedom is to be found within our relationships, not outside them.

Freedom is found within relationships; independence is without

When we use the word 'person' about somebody we are saying something relational about this man or woman or child. The word 'person' belongs in the same group of relational terms as father, mother, daughter, son, brother, sister, partner, spouse, citizen, employer, customer, friend, and so on. All of these terms point beyond the individual and imply that they are in a relational bond with one or more other people. It also implies the existence of associated responsibility, of duties and rights. 'Person' points towards something more universal or unfocused about our relatedness than these other names. Freedom is a state which is experienced by persons. Therefore fulfilment as a person, in which freedom must play a part, can by definition be found only within our sense of relatedness.

It is important not to confuse freedom with independence. Independence is a counterfeit of freedom. A man, woman or child may try to break away from responsiveness to others into independence. But in this sort of independence we lose some facets of our personhood. I see many people in their forties who by chasing independence have ended up alone and lonely and trapped by the limits of their own personalities. The hopes they had based on independence have proved false. Dependency and independence are both traps. Freedom is to be found as we accept a *mutual inter-dependence* with others for our gathering and our giving.

By accepting our loss we can change it into the gift of life to others

Building depth into relationship is partly achieved through being honest about the feelings associated with our own losses and those of another. Without this honesty, what we are really doing as we go about life is to take part in a kind of parallel play, sometimes closer to and sometimes more distant from the other person. The 'sixty per cent loss' in relationship building may at first seem daunting, but it reduces to smaller and smaller proportions as we recognize, work through and accept our losses. As our losses turn into our gifts of life to others through deeper relatedness, so present experience and hope grow. The relationship will never be so fully built that there is no loss; but it can be built on such a firm foundation that losses are more rapidly accepted as the building goes on and on. Honesty about our feelings and the feelings of others are the doorways between our soul and theirs. There is something very beautiful about seeing a couple who obviously know each other well and respond to each other's emotion without even a word passing between them.

The importance of bargaining, negotiating, and taking turns

Building a relationship is bound to entail ongoing loss and this is one reason why it is important to understand the manner in which our yearning or longing to restore our losses makes us set about bargaining with others. There is more than one way of bargaining. The range of methods and options we have developed to bargain will significantly affect the type of relationships we are able to make.

Most of us are aware of the methods we have learnt to use in bargaining to get something we want, such as permission from those to whom we have responsibility to go away for a weekend with friends. These methods are similar to those we might use to limit or restore some loss we have experienced. Imagine, for example, how you might react if somebody announced they had cancelled a trip the two of you were going to share because they could no longer afford it. Would you set about agreeing to do something else together instead? Or would some argument or accusation follow as an expression of your loss? In this connection, it may be a pity that in western culture we have largely lost the bargaining attitude. Shop prices are fixed and there is a 'take it or leave it' attitude in buying and selling, which all too often can be seen also in our personal relationships. Perhaps we should attend more car boot sales and learn to exercise our bargaining skills, so that they do not degenerate into a fixed-price mentality, which is what happens in some marriages.

It is worth spending a little time imagining the techniques we might employ either to reduce the price of an item we want to buy at a car boot sale or to reduce the disappointment of some inter-personal loss in each of our most important relationships. Would we be active about bargaining, or passively accept the price quoted? Could we be too shy to ask, or become pushy or belligerent? What arguments might we muster to justify another attempt at a different type of weekend break at lower cost to ourselves? How far do we consider the situation of the seller in the way we set about bargaining? These questions are important in determining the depth of relationships we are able to build in all sorts of situations. The alternative is parallel play – take it or leave it.

Many business management courses are available which teach ways of refining bargaining skills. They tend to present them in the more positive language of 'negotiating'. Negotiating is a process where people are trying to *maximize gain* in a given situation, which is subtly different from the points I have been making up to now. I have been describing bargaining skills as the attempt to *minimize loss*. Negotiating skills courses encourage people to look for a win-win situation for all involved, rather than a win-lose or at its worst a lose-lose situation. There might be different negotiating aims in mind for business and for personal relationships, but the same principles of positive inter-personal bargaining apply in both situations. If the losses involved in negotiating balanced gains are denied rather than aired, then the loss reactions will come out sooner or later to cause unexpected trouble.

How might an inter-personal negotiation look in a home setting? My in-laws offer a good example. They are horticultural farmers who live and work together all the time, which many couples might find rather too intense. What has helped them is that fairly early in their relationship they negotiated an agreement that has been a successful stand-by for many years. My wife's mother said that what she most disliked was being taken for granted. My wife's father explained in turn that what he most disliked was being ignored. Knowing simply this much about each other, that loss of respect for the one and loss of attention for the other would count as great loss, has been a treasure of wisdom from which they and others have benefited greatly.

Obviously it is not possible to negotiate in building personal relationships unless people can be honest with each other about what would represent loss for them. Such honesty is risky, because it calls for a degree of trust, and if that trust were abused then hurt would follow. Yet apart from taking that risk of honesty and openness, our relationships would not be solid structures but more like two-dimensional plans which map out only how to avoid sources of danger. Our relationships would involve the wrong sort of negotiating, like a solo skier who manages to 'negotiate' the bends down a mountain slope and survives to reach the bottom, excited, but – alone.

But how do we set about negotiating in our personal relationships? The answer is one of those simple and obvious features of common sense which we easily forget. Family therapists observing children playing together have noticed that they often become disturbed if adults do not know when to let them get on and finish whatever they are engaged in, but constantly interrupt them. The adults may be trying to 'show an interest' but the children see it as an irrelevant distraction and intrusion. But children seem to respond very differently when they learn from adults how to take turns amongst themselves and with adults. It helps them to develop more balanced lives . . .

'First you, then me.' . . . 'First me, then you.' . . . 'What are you doing?' . . . 'This is what I am doing.' 'What are you hoping to see?' . . . 'This is going wrong for me' . . . 'This is what I feel about what happened . . . 'What do you feel about what has happened?' . . .

Taking turns is a simple dynamic. It works well with children. It works equally well amongst adults.

CHAPTER 9

Finding Time and Finding Words

To accept difference from others is fundamental loss

Relationships are among the most important aspects of our lives and closely linked to our feelings of gain and loss. When a relationship problem arises, there will almost certainly be some kind of loss reaction hiding somewhere. As long as these loss reactions remain unrecognized and unresolved the problem will remain unsolved. However, before two people 'find each other' again they have to overcome an unexpected difficulty.

Generally speaking, men and women approach relationships in different ways; unless this is both recognized and accepted they meet at a barrier instead of in a meeting place. A difficulty which can prevent people recognizing and accepting these differences arises if they confuse equality with sameness. Only things which are different can be equal. If they are not different they must be the same, not equal. When it comes to the issue of equality between women and men this confusion can be dangerous. Women's equality means that the differences between men and women must be equally valued on both sides of all sorts of personal and business relationships that men and women make, and valued just as much as are the differences among men and among women. But while it is true that men and women are increasingly doing the same things, this does not mean that women and men are the same. They are equally and obviously different in every single cell of their bodies that contain DNA, and these genetic differences bring about not only different bodily shapes and abilities, but also tendencies to respond differently to situations. It is not only in their responses that men and women differ but also in their expectations of outcome. For example, it is virtually unheard of for a man to think of repairing a difficult relationship by having another baby. Obviously there is a large overlap of behaviours and abilities between the sexes and so an apparent sameness in many situations; but in general, men and women do tend to be good at different things. There is something wrong with society if people are anxious to deny such differences.

Is there any possible explanation for the widespread denial of these differences? It is very likely connected with the fact that denial occurs when there is some element of loss. Accepting difference is, strange to say, one of the most fundamental of losses. It means losing the safe idea that I am a complete person alone.

To be a person is to be a unique 'individual of a people'. Personal identity requires there to be 'another' – 'I and Thou' as Martin Buber entitled his book, or 'me and you' to use more everyday English. To acknowledge how deep the difference is means that we must lose our self-contained completeness. See the anger of loss arise in racism, for example.

I believe the non-acceptance of this fundamental loss is the emotional root of the repression of women practised by men throughout history. I think equally the non-acceptance of the loss involved in difference is the emotional root of militant feminism. The way we treat our spouse or our opposite is an outward sign of the way we treat the deeper most missing or lost elements of our selves. When more marriages break down than which survive, this suggests that people are preferring denial of their incompleteness, alone, to facing the hurt that is involved in giving out of their depths to receive somebody else. It is a cliché to say that the grass looks greener in another field, but – as I heard a preacher say the other day – the grass truly is greener where we water it.

Many people are shocked out of a previous way of seeing life when they realize that in order to thrive they need other human beings who are different from them. If a desire to find sameness takes over, then a major loss reaction is on its way sooner or later. Occasionally I see tragic examples of this when people arrive in my GP office, disillusioned and lonely in their late thirties and early forties because, for all their lives so far, they have mistaken sameness for equality. Consequently they have tried to force somebody else to be like them – and have failed, and lost them.

Accepting two profound male-female differences

There are two profound differences between male and female psychology that I often find relevant in the surgery to help people through these difficult patches.

1. *The importance of presence*

Generally speaking, men tend to take a problem-solving approach to life. They ask themselves, 'What is the problem? What's the solution? Right – let's do it.' Women, on the other hand, tend to see life more in terms of the push and pull of relational networks. They tend to notice and value the qualities of context, time, and environments, and so they work to develop and maintain these. I am not saying that men and women *ought* to be this or that. These are different perspectives on life that both men and women have, but which on average each group tends to prefer. The tremendous overlap of perspectives between the sexes is actually valuable because it allows the flexibility which makes each relationship thrive and become uniquely different. But when a relationship runs into difficulties, then I am saying that the chances of finding a long lasting solution are much greater if each partner makes a shift in their stance that enhances this difference rather than denies it.

Because of this difference men often find it difficult to accept that for a woman the solution to the relationship problem she sees will, to a large extent, be found in a need to feel the presence of her man. Most men do not realize how much presence they have, nor how effective their presence is in building relational networks and qualities. They think they must be *doing* solutions to problems. If they cannot be doing anything or cannot understand the problem in terms of what they can do, then they feel useless. They feel that since they can do nothing to help, they might as well go somewhere where they can be doing something useful that they understand.

Men often have surprisingly poor self-regard for their own presence. Their unrecognized losses of effectiveness in the past may have left them with this depressive delusion that they are useless. It does not come naturally to many men to know that if a woman feels loss then he may not need to say or do anything other than be a positive presence for her. If a man doesn't understand this he may keep at a distance, and while he is 'absent' in this way, will likely feel undervalued. This makes the woman feel abandoned and also undervalued because she cannot make her man happy enough to stay around. Failing to recognize this difference, or undervaluing it, creates a hidden ferment which is likely, sooner or later, to give rise to trouble.

There is loss in this difference of approach, because each person is incomplete and does not have the whole truth or is is right alone. If it is denied rather than accepted it emerges later when the man's loss of self-respect and the woman's loss of his presence becomes acute. However, true creative acceptance of the loss inherent in this difference turns it into a valuable gift of each to the other. Then they can, for example, live out the truth that a home is created by a woman's touch and a man's word. If one is missing then both lose.

2. The important difference between love and admiration

The second difference is this. The feeling of fulfilment and freedom that a woman has when she knows she is *loved* is one and the same as the feeling that a man has when he knows he is *admired*. It is a common saying that love makes the world go round, but not entirely true on its own. Things go round if two different forces are applied in different directions to different parts. Relationships between men and women get into a creative spin because men and women have, in general, different emotional needs that are fulfilled in different ways. It is love combined with a good regard of another that makes the world go round. The two genders differ in their preference for these. Recognizing the difference helps us to give life.

Problems may arise in building sustainable relationships where women are trying to be admired and men are trying to be loved. Correspondingly, problems may arise if women behave in ways that are not loveable and if men behave in ways that are not admirable.

The desire for sameness between the genders creates difficulties in this area as well. When a problem arises in a relationship a woman may hope to restore it by showing love. The man aware he is in the midst of a problem, is quite likely to feel this as smothering. Likewise if a man wants to restore a relationship he may try to do so by showing admiration of his woman. Unfortunately she is likely to feel this to be despicable since he really ought to be getting on with the business of properly loving her. I emphasize again that I am not saying that men and women *ought* to be this or that. But I *am* saying that when a relationship runs into difficulty an enduring solution is much more likely if each values the other enough to decide to change in the direction that acknowledges these profound differences. If the woman can find anything to admire in her man, and if the man can find anything to love in his woman, these are the lights that will grow as the end of the dark tunnel approaches. One way of settling relationship difficulties is by sincerely agreeing to differ.

The importance of naming feelings as they bond our differences

In Chapter 3 the first main message of the book was stated:

> *To help somebody else through their grief you do not need to say anything, only choose to stick around sometimes and be a listening presence. That is showing true mercy.*

The second is:

> *If you are going to say something to help others adjust to loss, then first learn to name your own feelings.*

The importance of naming feelings cannot be emphasized enough. To restate a point made earlier, honesty about our feelings is the window into our soul, and the doorway into another's. Naming our feelings is the very basis of mental health, relational strength, and peace of heart. Naming feelings turns our thoughts away from the objects of life

towards the hearts of the people who are making life for us
and for whom we are making life. It's true that when two
people look each other in the eye and really meet
heart-to-heart words may become unnecessary. But most of
the time words are the means by which we create or destroy
life.

I have found that even highly educated people can have a
poor vocabulary for their own feelings and those of others'.
It is possible that some readers of this book may feel they
have only a very few words available to describe how they
feel. But because it strengthens the foundations of a relationship for people to practice naming their own feelings to
each other with as wide a vocabulary as possible, I have pre-
pared some word lists (with the assistance of *Roget's
Thesaurus*). They are structured around the seven loss
phases. They are by no means complete and you may wish
to add your own words. I found the list on 'acceptance' to
be almost ridiculous to prepare. In acceptance of loss all of
life is given to others and to us. The section would cover the
whole range of emotions and drives which describe how we
are all – as the Bible says – bound up together in the bundle
of life. In the end I decided that the list presented here under
'acceptance' is really a list of sub-headings that you might
like to use as starters for building up your own lists –
perhaps together with somebody else when this seems
appropriate.

Adolescence: encounters with loss

Another kind of difference-related loss often occurs as children grow into adolescence. At this point they are very
likely to become 'different'. One of the most difficult stages
for parents is when their adolescent children leave home as
adult sons and daughters. Being a person who is a parent

seems to imply that you should have 'children' bonded to you. But at this stage it all becomes quite complicated. Does the fact that they are now adults mean that I am no longer a parent? Or if I remain as a parent should I now have an adult bonded to me in the same way that my child was bonded? Or is it right instead that bonding should remain between me as an adult and my offspring as an adult? Sticking the labels on each other of 'child' and 'parent' seems unnecessary at this stage, and indeed could be crippling if by doing so it forces the other to continue behaving the way things were all those years ago. Perhaps to establish a true adult-to-adult relationship with your sons and daughters is one of the deepest expressions of the utter relatedness which is meant by being a person, including as it does the loving acceptance of simultaneous loss and gain.

It is usually not difficult to recognize the clues showing that our children are no longer children but adolescents. Less clear are the clues that our adolescents must no longer be thought of as adolescents, but adults. The difference may be this. Children becoming adolescents are usually activating new patterns of 'gathering'. Adolescents becoming adults, on the other hand, are usually converting loss reactions into true acceptance. They are incorporating these loss reactions into their overall understanding of life.

For example, adolescents often start to gather memorabilia of sport or entertainment heroes – or new experimental clothes – or personality models, as they match their personalities with others in a peer group. After a while, though, the differences between them begin to emerge as over the few years of adolescence their personalities develop other interests – or fail to do so. They experiment with breaking relationships as well as making them, hearing criticism from others and adjusting to it, choosing to apply themselves to something when their friends tempt them to do something else . . . All these partings of ways bring a hope of gain and a reality of loss in the short term. This can be paralysing, ignored, denied, bargained, or accepted. Apart from the general moodiness that accompanies the hormonal activation of adolescence, these loss reactions add an extra dimension which parents can find quite impenetrable. If parents follow the age-old advice of 'leave well alone until the hormones settle down' they may unwittingly fail to help a balanced adjustment in the area where they can greatly help – adjusting to losses so that we can learn to gather most effectively together. Loss reaction analysis can help families achieve insight about the problems for adolescents growing up, without having the atmosphere full of judgmental accusations that there has been some failing on either side.

The family meeting, or pow-wow

One method I recommend for this is to call an occasional 'family pow-wow'. Any name for it will do if that one sounds a bit odd. A family meeting is a time set apart from the normal habits and rules of the household. It is therefore very important that it has an identifiable start, and that it comes to a clear end so that the normal household rules are known to apply once again. During the meeting the normal rules of everyday life don't apply. Instead there are only two rules:

- everybody must try to name their feelings about the impact of somebody else's behaviour upon them, and use the formula, 'When you do . . ., I feel . . .';
- everybody must risk being completely honest even if they fear this level of honesty will hurt somebody else's feelings.

The formula, 'When you do . . ., I feel . . .' is very important. It does not come naturally to people, and GPs have to go on weekend courses to learn how to say it! The natural statement is this: 'When you do . . . it makes me feel . . .'. We all say it, because this statement shifts the blame for my subsequent reaction onto the other person! Unfortunately this shift is felt by that person as at least a push, if not a shove away. It is a rejecting statement, not a bonding statement. The alternative is to leave a bit of open space for thought in the middle of the statement, represented by the comma in the sentence after 'When you do . . . ,' Then the simple subsequent statement 'I feel . . .' becomes a bond. It is clearly saying that I move as you move but I am not going to be ruled by you. It shifts some *responsibility* back onto the other person, but without an inflammatory sense of blame . . .

Calling an end to the meeting is important. For some families the meeting may be an enjoyable time, but for many it will be full of risk as the adolescents experiment with communicating their feelings and the adults experiment with losing their impressions. Normal daily living may come to seem a safer option. The depth of communication in a meeting can then be allowed to gradually stimulate adjustments to the losses of image, illusion and hope that accompany growing up and bring insight into our differences. If families make use of the meeting and learn through it how the loss reaction analysis can help to build relationships during times of change rather than break them, then it can become a most valuable part of the family inheritance.

The three main points to remember

The final sentence this book makes the point that we may fear people will have a judgmental attitude towards us at some encounters or meetings, when in fact the meetings are more about discovering how far we can trust giving freedom to each other to build a relationship. The fear of loss of face, feeling shocked about shaming, may make us get the whole thing upside down. Thus discovering how we can talk about the possibilities for creativity while knowing and accepting our limits is an important feature of freedom. A whole person is incomplete alone, so we all have limits alone and we all overcome them by discovering freedom with each other. We can avoid letting talk about loss from becoming morbid and self centred if we learn the skills to recognize when loss is affecting relationships and well-being, so that we can react appropriately to help people see and bridge across their limits. Three points can guide us towards naming what we recognize so that we can respond better. Two of the points have already been mentioned:

1. *To help somebody else through their grief you do not need to say anything, only choose to stick around sometimes and be a listening presence. That is showing true mercy.*
2. *If you are going to say anything to help others adjust to any of their losses, then first learn to name your own feelings.*

Now we can add the third main point of the book:

3. *If you recognize that what you yourself feel is one of the loss reaction emotions, then before you say anything else, first name to yourself what it is that you are afraid you might lose in this dialogue.*

If you skip over this third point, the chances are that you will react in a way that stops the other person exploring their limits and how to overcome them with you. If instead you can 'count to ten' while you remain silent and reflect on what you have to lose here, and which stage of the loss reaction you feel about that risk now, then you will be opening doors to another's soul in the midst of that silence. Out of that silence can form a spoken bond which is stronger than mere words. It is by naming our own fears of loss that we come to a deeper self-knowledge and a stronger sense of our own identity so that we can sustain our place in a true relationship.

Silently, inwardly, I have watched people grow in strength and stature in the surgery as they let go of fears. I have seen the addict admitting their plight to a parent and feeling their forgiveness instead of the dreaded rejection from parents who already knew but were too afraid to say; the bulimic admitting her fear of losing her boyfriend – and gaining one instead; the businessman admitting his fear of forgetting his lines in a presentation – and learning instead to talk to the heart of the matter; the man admitting his fear of growing old alone – and gaining a new relationship with his son.

Our hopes, dreams and plans and activity express only half our identity, the gathering half; to build sustainable relationships in which we know the freedom to become whole together we must learn to take the risk of sharing our fears of loss as well. Having done this we can really know we have met another person, when they do not abuse that knowledge but open up life instead. We will have found our own personal place among our people.

*   *   *   *   *

Appendix: Naming feelings

SHOCK

regret	unreal	apprehension
numb	unexpected	jitters
low	unprepared	dread
shaken	horror	fright
agitated	cold sweat	terror
anxious	dismay	alarm
sudden rush	restless	unaccounted for
omen	distant	scared
staggered	surprise	panic
if only	thunderbolt	shiver
disorientated	bombshell	hysterical
sudden	jolt	out of control
confused	flap	tremble

DENIAL

ignore	rebuff	refuse
irrelevant	reject	disbelieve
insignificant	turn a deaf ear	contradict
detachment	not want	lie
indifference	disallow	disown
negate	harden one's heart	disclaim
refute	revoke	separate
rebut	dismiss	turn away
dissent	never	withhold
invalidate	gone away	disavow
repulse	not possible	decline

ANGER

resentment	hate	rivalry
bitterness	implacable	vexation
irritation	unappeasable	possessiveness
fury	animosity	sullenness
passion	grudge	sulk
rage	vindictiveness	reprisal
wrath	revengefulness	vendetta
dudgeon	spite	avenge
rancour	malice	virulence
soreness	malevolence	jealousy
indignation	sore point	envy
offence	dangerous subject	temper
gall	aggravation	distrust

GUILT

remorse	own up	lost
questioning	transgression	liable
blame	trespass	regret
culpability	omission	mortified
involvement	frailty	soul searching
complicity	feebleness	self-reproach
charge	weakness	contrite
onus	humanity	apologize
reproach	imperfect	penitent
bad conscience	fault	disillusioned
suspicion	flawed	repentant
desire to confess	divided	rueful

BARGAINING

Aggressive	Assertive	Passive
take	what if?	concede
make a stand	bid	longing
feud	restore	defeatism
threat	redeem	nostalgia
gamble	if . . . then . . .	non-action
vendetta	ransom	paralysed
corner	speculate	inert
poison	risk	play dead
aggressor	assert	passivity
high pressure	negotiate	low pressure
repress	discuss	apathetic
dominate	invest	stagnate
drive	attempt	keep latent
head-on	try to	wait and see
challenge	state	smoulder
leverage	declare	lie low
pull one's weight	influence	procrastinate
claim	venture	resign
allure	appeal	sufferance
mesmerize	attract	put off
coolness	composure	endurance
fascinate	tolerance	meekness
compel	affect	acquiesce
prevail upon	convince	fight shy
impress	persuade	submit
work upon	motivate	vegetate
induce	inspire	step back
break	transform	be moulded
stoicism	steadiness	hesitancy

DEPRESSION

sadness	out of sorts	unnerved
meaningless	sluggish	unconfident
melancholy	listless	unassured
darkness	mournful	downcast
alienated	lamenting	crestfallen
forbidding	wretched	subdued
withdrawn	moody	heavy-hearted
shut off	sulky	sick at heart
suppressed	sullen	solemn
hopeless	glum	humourless
aimless	care worn	uncongenial
miserable	disappointed	uninviting
useless	dejected	dull
despondent	joyless	flat
defeated	unhappy	dismal
pessimistic	dreary	gloomy
unlively	dispirited	sombre

ACCEPTANCE

dignity	kindness	liberation
fruitfulness	goodness	harmony
bearing affliction	gentleness	purity
perseverance	faithfulness	freedom
character	self-control	consideration
hope	truthfulness	impartiality
understanding	forgiveness	sincerity
faith	grace of giving	generosity
integrity	justice	fulfilment
love	mercy	rest
joy	reconciliation	submitting one to another
peace	flourishing	prosperity of heart
patience	healing	maturity

CHAPTER 10

Spirituality and Giving-Receiving

Looking for wholeness rather than problems

The central idea of this book is that at every stage in life we are liable to have experiences of 'loss'. Other people may perceive them as important or trivial, but this has very little to do with how we ourselves feel about them. We have seen that the ways in which we react to these experiences have a good deal in common with the way in which people respond to bereavement. One might almost say – although with perhaps some exaggeration – that living as a human being involves us in a series of small deaths. (Some of them, of course, may be so devastating that they may feel almost like death itself.) It's not only the coward who – as Shakespeare said – 'dies many time before his death'.

We have considered how and why we should face the risk of talking with others about what hurts us. Doing this is risky because it means giving people the information they could use to hurt us more if they chose. On the other hand, when we choose to make ourselves vulnerable in this way by talking about what we would be afraid to lose, we are in fact laying the foundation on which to build true relationships. When we have a true relationship we cannot lose all.

Thinking about our experiences in this way may have led us to focus unduly on the problems of life. But no matter how overwhelming they may seem, there is more to life than solving problems. In this chapter I want to re-focus our attention on how accepting the inevitability of some loss can help us, instead, to become wholeness-orientated, and more creative. In fact, when we live in acceptance of loss in general, and of our own losses in particular, we will actually find ourselves becoming better givers of life to others and receivers of that which others likewise need to give. That giving and receiving is part of being a unique person in a community of people. Living to give and receive, and the spirit in which it is done, are the real face of the hidden inter-relatedness of life that some people call their spirituality.

So in this final chapter we are going to look at how we can come to terms with the biggest loss of all, the one that there is no way of escaping and the one that we are most unwilling to think about – our own mortality. For the sober truth is that each of us is going to die sooner or later. I said in the first chapter that science and entertainment have little positive to say about death, but I also claimed that if we look instead at the language of relationship building and spirituality then we shall learn a great deal which will be positive and of lasting value – not mere platitudes but solid truths. We shall find that as we come to terms with our own mortality we shall become more creative. There should be nothing surprising about this, because by facing reality in this way we shall be orientating ourselves towards wholeness.

Our spirituality is 'who we tend to listen to'

People who normally have nothing to do with religion may find themselves praying when confronted with the risk of losing someone they love. We should not deny the significance of this 'spiritual' feature of our humanity. If we deny the drive to pray we are on the verge of losing even our humanity.

Some think prayer and spirituality are merely wishful thinking – a safety net for escape when we cannot face up to life. They see prayer and spirituality as a denial of reality. This may in part be because they realize that they tend to think less about prayer during the gathering phase of the life cycle, and more about it during the loss phase. But I don't see prayer like that at all. I believe the drive to pray is a sign of the extent to which we as human beings are built to be knit together in relationships. Relatedness is utterly fundamental to the way we see life. Expecting there to be someone to listen and to listen to is part of the human level of reality we are dealing with in this book. I would even go so far as to say that our spirituality is, in effect, 'who we tend to listen to'.

Seen in this way, spirituality is an everyday feature of life for all of us. Humanists, who are usually thought of as rejecting spirituality, do have it in one sense, because they believe in listening to and building relationships with the people they can hold and see. People who read – and so listen to – those who write their horoscopes have another sort of spirituality because they believe our relationship with the changing cosmos speaks into our daily lives. New Agers have another sort of spirituality because they believe we listen intuitively to Nature within us and so build a relationship with Mother Earth. Hindus and yogis have another sort of spirituality because they believe that through the objects of this world we build relationships with different levels of deity. Spiritualists and people from many tribal religions have another sort of spirituality because they believe we listen to ancestral spirits. The spiritualities of Christians, Jews and Muslims have a common belief that human beings can listen with their inner hearts to a

Supreme Being who makes all of life personal. Christians and Jews believe this God relates creatively with each human being individually. And so it goes on. Everybody, including atheists and materialists, have their own sort of 'spirituality', because everybody believes in the existence of somebody else to listen to.

Each person prays in whatever way makes sense to them, in hope, in faith, in love. That is why everybody can find themselves praying when confronted with the risk of loss. Different prayers are appropriate in different settings – the silent prayer of appeal, the quiet tearfulness of hope, the formal prayer, the ritual prayer, the staying with when we would rather go, the comforting hand to hold, the look that says 'I value you enough to give you time'. Prayer is listening and speaking from our inner heart, rather than from our senses and mind. If we deny that our inner heart has any impact on life then we will not pray. That is why we risk losing our humanity if we deny the drive to pray.

The benefits of accepting our own mortality

One of the most challenging situations in which we discover the depth or otherwise of our own wholeness is when we are faced with the need to comfort someone else who is grieving over the death of a loved one. Doing this is extremely difficult until we have truly accepted the fact that we ourselves are going to die. Learning to comfort does not mean simply learning to be soft. Becoming a comforter is one and the same as learning to know the other person; and for that we have to overcome denial within ourselves.

We can creatively overcome denial of our own mortality by using the seven stages of loss reactions to look at ourselves; the method should by now have become very familiar.

Most people live some of their lifetime in *denial* of the fact that they themselves are going to die. At some point we all emerge from this denial to feel shock at the idea that it could all end when our lives end. Shock involves doubt that we have the resources to make the most of living now, or perhaps even in some future life if there proves to be one. This doubt brings a fear of being overwhelmed – for some, by the effects of the past and for others by the demands of the present or future; either can bring anxiety about how to cope with the next few moments. To see these fears, doubts and anxieties as clues to our own loss reactions can help us all find ways to overcome our denial of our own mortality. We do this by carefully assessing just what our resources really are to handle each stage of the loss reactions involved. It is, as we shall see, the process of forgiving which is being stretched out into workable stages – forgiving others, God and oneself.

Some have progressed out of denying their own mortality into *anger* about it. This is sometimes expressed in a 'devil-may-care' attitude that sees life as meaningless, and all moral principles as empty words, since everything about us is destined to return to dust. It may lead to an 'eat, drink and be merry, for tomorrow we die' lifestyle, but sadly it may also drive some people to grapple with life with an intensity that can have disastrous consequences. For exam-ple, 'take what you can get' is a very different attitude to 'make use of opportunities'. 'Taking' can be a cover for abuse of others when they have not chosen to 'give' an opportunity. Wilful abuse of others has an evil effect in their lives, which can take many years of counselling to untangle. It is very difficult for an abusive person, or one whose habit-ual stance is mockery or ridicule, to give any comfort to another who is bereaved.

Others have progressed from denial of their own mortal-ity into *guilt*. Guilty shame drives some people to try to lead perfect lives; it can also drive some to accuse other people of not leading perfect lives. Guilt makes us reach for the 'cover-up', and then that false sense of security becomes its own trap. From within it we become judgmental; and while it's true that we all need to exercise judgement to be wise, it is often not wise for us to 'pass judgement' without first learning a little more about ourselves. Learning to be gentle with ourselves is often a hard lesson, and the idea that this can be a stepping stone towards true acceptance of our own mortality may not appear to make sense. But it is as human beings that we die, having helped each other together through our imperfections. Perfect works of art, like statues, never die, and may not give much comfort to the bereaved either.

In the secrecy of their hearts many people *bargain* with God about death. This is probably a very healthy way of living – provided we do not tie ourselves up in impossible conditions. This is the sad plight which some health faddists get into, following the latest advice from experts on diet and exercise even though one author may contradict another. The man who popularized jogging as a form of exercise, died of a heart attack in his fifties – on a run. Unfortunately those who are young at heart may feel that 'moderation in all things' is not an inspiring way of life. Perhaps, 'bargaining: in all things giving and receiving,' is a better one. It can apply both to gathering the good experiences and friendships that make our life, and equally to giving time to comfort others when they are bereaved.

Some people who have emerged from denial of their own mortality have been able to progress only as far as a sense of *powerlessness and meaninglessness* about their existence. This may be experienced in the despair which switches on when the television is switched off. It has been called an 'existential depression'. Life is an empty void which no amount of stimulation or effort can fill. This response may underlie carelessly self-destructive behaviours such as smoking or the abuse of alcohol and drugs. It may tolerate injustice. It may distance the suffering of others from oneself. It is a God-shaped hole-in-the-heart. And, just like the others, this state of mind is one which makes it difficult to comfort another who is bereaved, since it shows that we ourselves have not yet fully accepted our own mortality.

To get a clear and creative picture of what it could be like to have fully accepted our mortality we must go back to first principles. True *acceptance* of our mortality must, according to first principles, be a very rich and mature state of mind, not a hopeless and empty one. Acceptance must include not only an awareness of our powerlessness but also a realistic hope. Anything short of that is not true acceptance. To go one step further, accepting our own mortality means realizing that our death is indeed a complete ending over which we are powerless, while equally realizing that even in our death there must be hope of renewal of some different sort of creative life. To miss out on either of these two is to side-step true acceptance of our mortality.

If we somehow side-step that full range of acceptance, we lose some benefit that true acceptance would have on the way we live with others now. The reactions from that hidden loss will have their way, and should be identifiable in our behaviour with others if we look for them.

What happens when we side-step true acceptance of death

Talking with people about death in the GP's office is as natural as talking about life. Neither is easy, but both can be equally rewarding in terms of building lasting relationships. It is an obvious point, but nevertheless worth making, that people picture the ending and the renewal of life very differently. For example, many see it as the continuing cycle of birth of the next generation to which they will have left some lasting benefit of experience or resources. Some people, though, who are depressed to the point of considering suicide, sadly distort their despair into a hope that they will be in oblivion while others would be better off without them. On the other hand, some hope not for oblivion but to experience their own continuing personal existence in another world, leading to reincarnation later in this world. Others hope for a shared perfection of heaven with a new and eternally different body. Most commonly people vaguely feel that a mixture of these may be true, without having any clear ideas. Honest lack of certainty is no stumbling block to mentally airing our emotions about our own death. But if we avoid thinking about it, we may find those hidden emotions are making our ideas drift towards one of two extremes. Either of these is in effect a way of side-stepping true acceptance of our mortality. (But there is also a middle path which as a doctor I see people learn to walk with improving balance.)

One extreme is to see our death as annihilation without hope. This is a desperate state that few people would think it reasonable to aim for. The hopelessness of this state could open the way to a breakdown of moral values. People would find themselves concerned only about self and the here and now. It is possible that if increasing numbers of people follow this pattern of failed acceptance of the reality of death, society may break apart into competitive self-centredness, the modern jungle. Are we perhaps seeing some of this in contemporary western post-modern culture? This extreme is not acceptance of death but flight from it.

The opposite extreme is to side-step true acceptance by hoping that there will be no ending at all. Throughout history and in all cultures this is the more usual extreme which people may opt for or drift into. The good thing about it is that it preserves a sense of the value of life, something that I do not in any way wish to injure. What I do want to do, however, is to show how this view can be enriched by accepting that death is a real ending, a complete stop and change affecting all of our nature, a separation from the way we know – or think – things to be. Recognizing this becomes less painful and shocking for oneself and others when there is an equally real hope for the renewal of the whole person, body, soul and spirit – if that is the best way to see human existence. But to imagine that some aspect of our nature, such as our soul, will pass though death completely unchanged by the process leaves out something very important. For even if our personal nature is eternal, and we could call this nature our 'name' to avoid confusion, then all the parts of our nature which together are included in that name must experience some change together. Dispersion of the body would be accompanied by a change of the soul from one type of glory to a different type; and this change as it affects our relatedness means loss of the old, *before* gain of the new. Believing there will be no ending at all, no loss of the old in change, may be an extreme to which people side-step without realizing how doing so could be a flight from death rather than an acceptance of it.

Shakespeare described movingly how the uncertainty about the nature of this change does bring fear about death. He did so in the words Hamlet speaks as he contemplates suicide, starting with that famous question, 'To be, or not to be?'

> . . . To die, to sleep –
> . . . perchance to dream: ay, there's the rub;
> For in that sleep of death what dreams may come,
> When we have shuffled off this mortal coil,
> Must give us pause . . .
> For who would bear the whips and scorns of time . . .
> But that the dread of something after death, –
> The undiscover'd country, from whose bourn

No traveller returns, – puzzles the will,
And makes us rather bear those ills we have
Than fly to others that we know not of?

Hamlet could cope with the trials of his life because he had
had an experience – the encounter with his father's ghost –
which had convinced him of the reality of something
personal beyond, and greater, than this world. He had a
reasonable hope, awesome though it was, which is difficult
for us if we have not had any such experience ourselves.
Hearing about other people's experiences is not quite the
same, but I will try to show in the next section of this chapter how we can glimpse something similar in our everyday
lives which might act as the seed of such a reasonable hope. I
want to show that there are reasonable grounds to believe
we do have the resources to overcome any fear of that
change which might arise in our hearts.

Both these two types of flight from death – anticipating
annihilation without hope of creative renewal, and cherish-
ing an unrealistic hope for no change at all – agree in *denying*
one aspect of the finality of death's change. Denial pushes
our emotions into the deep-freeze or – if you prefer the meta-
phor – sends them to sleep. Denial also brings fear when we
doubt our resources to cope. This fear can make us protective of our hibernating or deep-frozen emotions, and this
protectiveness can lead people in two different directions,
which are each in effect seeking the false security of opposing
factions in life. For example, some people show a great deal
of emotional force in expressing anti-religious feelings,
while others display an equal degree of emotion in their
anti-science stance. Could it be that, rather than meeting in
mutual enrichment as they accept their differences, this attitude of conflict is in fact driven by a release of the denied
emotions trapped in our flight from the risks of death. (The
idea may seem far-fetched, but think about it.) Whereas

people of different beliefs, any sort of beliefs, who have genuinely accepted the real change of their mortality and that of others, they have the potential to comfort each other in bereavement and thus minimize the loss caused by death. It is when we are caught in denial that the resurfacing of emotions such as anxiety, angry drives to change others, guilty self-doubt or powerlessness may hinder reconciliation at this most important time.

What happens when we find a middle path

We gain balance, some might call it poise instead of posing, when we walk a middle path between these two extreme flights from death. This middle path is walked by those who have learned to hope for a special type of renewal after the end of all we know. It is called resurrection – a word that people often do not understand in an everyday sense and therefore do not make use of as they could. It needs freshening up a bit. In this sense, resurrection is the concept that our life can know complete renewal on hearing the word of someone else who loves us and calls us by name.

If you recall the gospel stories about people being raised from the dead by Jesus, you will understand what I am getting at. Think, for example, of Mark 5 where Jesus brings Jairus' daughter back to life; or the story of the young man from Nain in Luke 7; and then there's the account of the raising of Lazarus in John 11. There are important differences between the stories but in each of them Jesus speaks directly to the dead person. His words to the little girl sound rather like her elder brother might have said to her any morning, 'Come on little girl, get up!' And he called Lazarus from the grave by name.

That *sort of* renewal can also be seen in lesser ways in our everyday living with each other, when we call to each other and show each other the sort of love which conveys renewed freedom to live. The way we speak to each other and the names we call each other can spread either darkness or light in each other's lives. We have that choice. In Christian teaching full resurrection is the way we overcome the extreme loss of death, but this ultimate example is not the only way in which the concept of resurrection is relevant to our lives and the lives of those we relate to. We need to take hold of this truth about 'resurrection' and see in it a way in which we can bring life to others.

The point is that resurrection-type renewal is something we all can participate in every day. Even if we doubt what life is all about, are clumsy with words, and have disagreements with those we know and comfort, we all can be speakers in pure love, callers by name, comforters of those we know. We can receive this from others and give them the hope of such renewal. Whatever it may be that they have lost or that they realize they will lose, is gone. But in spite of this they can still know they have unity of spirit with those who stick around, and in that their hope is made reality. The truth of this message is taken to its ultimate in the way of life that Jesus prayed people would aspire to. Such a way of life releases strength when the acceptance that our death is utterly final comes packaged with the acceptance that death is also no longer a trap. Realizing this does not supply us with some kind of short cut. We still need to go through the complex loss reactions of truly accepting that death is utterly final, but by doing this we shall ensure that our hope for renewal is realistic, as the power of ultimate resurrection becomes real here and now. Such a hope can give us a good reason to learn how to creatively give freedom in the lives of others we mix with every day.

Resurrection on calling by name is an immense creative force. At one level it is the creative power that drove the great reformers, for example, to confront the injustices of poverty and child labour in Victorian times against the interests of big business. At another, it is the same power that creates all the small and hidden acts of generosity which turn our streets into communities, and our houses into homes. That is how renewal takes living form along the middle path. That is how the strange Christian message of death and hope of resurrection is relevant to everyday losses and gains. Love-born hope continually calls us to reconciliation at heart despite disagreements in our ideas and minds. We must be honest; the disagreements are real and painful. How do we overcome them so as to achieve reconciliation? The answers have already been given. We need to learn the pattern of our personal difficulty in handling our own loss reactions, and then spend time thinking about the other person. What is their personality profile, their pattern of handling losses? And what represents loss for them? Name those losses underlying the feelings as precisely as possible. When we know this, we will be well on the way to becoming givers of life.

In what ways is this love-born hope stronger than either of the two extremes of denial we looked at earlier? We have seen how 'annihilation without hope' can lead to a modern jungle-type mentality. On the other hand, hoping that there will be no ending or change to an eternal part of our nature may lead some people to act as if everything about themselves and their community now, in the present, is an imperfection or a contamination, a problem imposed on the pure part of their nature. It is almost inevitable that such an attitude will devalue life here and now – perhaps to a disastrous extent. It can alienate people from all that is beautiful about sharing our humanity with others – even with people who are 'difficult'. It can lead us to see life too much in terms of the problems they face. It can nurture a hope focused on future escape from these problems, rather than a hope envisaging strength to overcome the difficulties of here and now.

Love-born hope based on a heart-to-heart call, on the other hand, enables us to live in the knowledge of beauty despite all that would mar it and make us forget it.

At the extremes we tend to see life as consisting of problems, while the middle path leads us to see life as possibilities. The difference is summed up in a brief, anonymous poem which I find very moving. Slowing down enough to think about it is almost like swallowing a pill.

> Two men looked out through prison bars.
> One saw mud, and the other the stars.

Love-born hope is strong because it is gives us reason enough to explain how we can know resurrection when we hear and respond to the call of one who loves us. This applies when we have truly accepted that we are going to die, and it is valid as much in our everyday living as in the utter ending of death. That hope is a hope worth sharing, and a real inheritance for the future generation.

In conclusion: we find ourselves and are found when we can give and receive the gift of true freedom

True freedom is the openness to behave in which we are known and are knowing of others, forgiven and forgiving of others. We experience it when we come out of hiding in the shadows of our independence and allow our loss reactions to be healed as we build relationships characterized by mutual knowledge and acceptance. We achieve freedom when we do for others as we would have done for ourselves – bringing healing and creativity.

This can be the quality of our everyday life, a life rich with a spirituality that is not just other-worldly, but here and now. Sometimes the risk can seem too great. We have put together our nest in the shadows and we are frightened to leave it. We are afraid that others may not respond in the way that supports our need to change. Even so, the hope remains realistic, and we need to sustain it.

We have been thinking about loss and reconciliation as they affect us individually. It may help us to take a broader view for a moment. However we understand God to be, the crucifixion of Jesus can show us that humanity's Godhead also knows the grief of loss and the joy of reconciliation, as a Father knows the loss of a Son he gave to us, and his return. Beyond anything we can ever imagine, this Godhead knows and shares all the feelings of grief that are involved in building relationships over time, with us who repeatedly turn our backs on God in just the same way that we may also turn it on each other.

Every year on Good Friday, when Christianity remembers why Jesus died, the Eastern Orthodox Church preaches the same message of hope. Their liturgy tells how humankind is destined to have a relationship with God that lasts even through and beyond the grave. In fact, that grave is where we each, alone, shall be found by God, whom we can meet with a joyful recognition when he calls our name and we respond like lovers who give their lives to each other in secret.

As we open our minds and hearts to this, we can begin to learn more about coming to terms with our human emotions of feeling trapped, and alone, and in pain, and powerless, which arise from having to bear the burden of our own mortality and the mini-deaths of the day's disappointments. Why should it help if we open our hearts to a hope of resurrection at the call of one who loves us? It is because that meeting in the grave will – as our meetings with people now could be – not be *basically* about judgment. It will be about trusting God as we begin to recognize the freedom God is to give us, and gives us now, within the fullness of our utter relatedness.